HUMAN ORIGINS AND DEVELOPMENT FROM AN AFRICAN ANCESTRY

A Review of Cultural Theory from the Beginning

Vol. 1 of a 2 Vols. set.

HUMAN ORIGINS AND DEVELOPMENT FROM AN AFRICAN ANCESTRY

HUMAN ORIGINS AND DEVELOPMENT FROM AN AFRICAN ANCESTRY

A Review of Cultural Theory from the Beginning
Vol. 1 of a 2 Vols. set.

by Gerhard Kraus

KARNAK HOUSE

First published in Britain 1990
by Karnak House
300 Westbourne Park Road
London W11 1EH, UK

British Library Cataloguing in Publication Data

Kraus, Gerhard
    Human origins & development from an African ancestry:
    a review of cultural history from its beginnings
    1. Culture, history
    I. Title
    909

    ISBN 0-907015-47-6
    ISBN 0-907015-48-4 pbk

Printed in Great Britain by Billing and Sons Ltd, Worcester.

ACKNOWLEDGEMENTS

During the several years of preparation preceding the publication of this slender volume thanks are due to the following personalities for their encouraging comments and constructive criticisms:

Dr. Jonathan Benthall, Director, Royal Anthropological Institute, London, Britain.

Prof. Allan Bilsborough, Dept. of Anatomy, University of Durham, Britain.

Prof. Emeritus George F. Carter, Dept. of Geosciences, Texas A&M University, USA.

The late Prof. Raymond Dart, Dept. of Anatomy, University of the Witwatersrand, Johannesburg, S.A.

Prof. Michael Day, Prominent British Anatomist, St. Thomas Hospital, London, Britain.

Prof. Ainsworth Harrison, Dept. Biological Anthropology, University of Oxford, Britain.

Dr. Jacquetta Hawkes, Archaeologist, Britain.

The late Prof. Edmund Leach, Dept. of Social Anthropology, University of Cambridge, Britain.

James Mellaart, Dept. of West Asian Studies, Institute of Archaeology, London, Britain.

Dr. P.R.S. Moorey, Archaeologist, Ashmolean Museum, Oxford, Britain.

Prof. Emeritus John L. Sorenson, Dept. of Anthropology, Breigham Young University, Utah, USA.

Prof. Phillip V. Tobias, Dept. of Anatomy, University of the Witwatersrand, Johannesburg, S.A.

Dr. Helen Whitehouse, Archaeologist, Ashmolean Museum, Oxford, Britain.

Prof. Bernard Wood, Dept. of Anthropology, University of Liverpool, Britain.

Prof. Colin Turnbull, Dept. of Anthropology, Vassar College, USA.

Prof. Fred Wendorf, Dept. of Anthropology, South Methodist University, USA.

Dr. Werner Kaiser, Egyptologist, German Archaeology Institute, Cairo, Egypt.

Dr. G. Dreyer, Egyptologist, German Archaeology Institute, Cairo, Egypt.

Dr. Stephen Quirke, Egyptologist, Egypt Dept., British Museum, London, Britain.

Special thanks for their continuous support during preparation are due to Dr. Joan Covey, Author on Anthropology, California, USA.; Tertius Chandler, Anthropologist, Berkeley, California; Rafique A. Jairazbhoy, Historian, Discoverer of extensive Egyptian links between Egypt and pre-Columbian America presently, Karachi, Pakistan, and Clayton E. Joel, deceased, Anthropologist and for twelve years editor of *Historical Diffusionism* (formerly *The New Diffusionist*), Potton, Britain.

'We are so much agreed that man emerged from Africa in the first place and that it would be ironic if we were wrong. All the evidence points that way: almost all the hominids and artefact sites over a million years old have been found in Africa; several lines of genetic evidence show man's close affinities with the African apes. But already around a million years ago occupation has undoubtedly spread out around the Old World, through Europe and Asia, and in much of those areas there is approximately archaeological continuity thereafter.'

'Out of Africa' (From John Gowlett's *The Coming of Modern Man*, in *Antiquity*, No. 61, 1987; pp 211[nd]212).

'The theory of cultural evolution, to my mind, is the most inane, sterile and pernicious theory ever conceived in the history of science (a cheap toy for the amusement of big children) ... Culture cannot be forced into a straight-jacket of any formulae. All that the practical investigator can hope for, at least for present, is to study each cultural phenomenon as exactly as possible in its geographical distribution, its historical development and its relation or association with kindred ideas.'

'Cultural Evolution' (From Berthold Laufer, in a review of Lowie's *Culture and Ethnology*, in *American Anthropology*, 1918, 20; 87/90)

Dedication

This work is dedicated to the late Professor Raymond A. Dart (1893–1988), famous for the discovery of Australopithecus, an event basic in the history of Human Evolutionary Studies. Dart's view that Africa was the cradle of humankind, now gradually accepted, took a long time to make headway against the Asia school of thought.

Portrait of Raymond A. Dart and the Taung child, painted by Alma Flynn of Johannesburg in 1983, on the occasion of Professor Dart's 90th birthday.

Commenting on a previous draft of the first part of the present work, Professor Dart wrote: 'I have gone through your manuscript, which I found deeply interesting and even enthralling. I had no idea that anyone had the breadth and vision you display. I trust that there are a sufficient number of people in both Europe and North America who are widely educated and sympathetic to your fundamental theses. What a magnificent understanding you have for humanity's past.'

CONTENTS

Glossary

Acheulian – The tradition of tool-making distinguished by hand-axes, with a duration of from c. $1^{1}/_{2}$ million years ago to c. 30,000 B.P.

Alleles – Genes which can mutate one to another, which occupy the same relative position (locus) on homologous chromosomes, and which undergo paring during meiosis.

Artefact – Any object fashioned for use by man.

Asymmetrical – Having the two sides unlike.

Aurignacian – Major Upper Palaeolithic tradition of Europe from c. 34,000 years B.P. to c. 27,000 B.P., characterized by long retouched blades, scrapers and split-base bone points. (See also Chapter 5, Part 1.)

Australopithecus (A.) – The earliest defined genus of hominid. (Almost all specimens occur in the time-range of between 4.0–1.3 million years ago.) The following species have been named:

A. afarensis – early form in Ethiopia.

A. africanus – early form in Southern Africa.

A. robustus – later robust form from S. Africa.

A. boisei – formerly Zinanthropus, also S. Africa.

Bantu – East Africans who speak languages of a single stock, so named.

Bipedalism – The habit of walking on two feet.

Blade – A parallel sided blade of flint of nearly uniform thickness.

Brain –

Wernike area: Controls speech

Broca area: Controls the muscular movements for sound.

Burin – A flint chisel.

Bushmen – (Considered by some a derogatory term.) Generally referring to the Khoi-San, aboriginal hunter-gatherers of South Africa.

Cenozoic – Same as Tertiary.

Cerbellum – Part of the brain projecting backwards.

Cerebellum – A special part of the brain projecting at back – 'little brain'.

Cerebral hemispheres – The different parts of the brain.

Cerebrum – Front part of the brain.

Chopper – A crude core of flint or other stone, sharpened by retouching along a single edge.

Chopping tool – The same as a chopper, but retouched by striking alternative blows from either side.

Chromosomes – Thread shaped bodies, numbers of which occur in every nucleus of animal or plant cells.

Civilization – Sometimes defined as a Post-Neolithic, complex society, mostly connected with a first appearance of kings and king-related gods, organized religion, monumental architecture, writing and a calendar.

Clactonian – An early flake industry from south-east England.

Cladogenesis – The branching off of evolutionary variations from the main-stem.

Cleaver – A form of biface tool found alongside the hand-axe on Acheulian sites especially in Africa.

Core (flint) – The central portion or nucleus of a flint nodule, formed by the removal of flakes or flake-blades.

Cortex – Outer part or rind; the grey matter of the brain.

Cultural Evolution – The belief that human culture progresses automatically from a low cultural level to one of greater complexity. Originally considered to be a continuation of biological evolution.

Darwinism – The transmutation of species by natural-selection (better called natural elimination). Darwin accepted part of Lamarckian heredity.

Dimorphic – Having two distinct forms.

Encephalisation – Enlargement of the brain substance.

Encephalon – The brain.

Endocast – Inner shape of the brain case, shown on a cast.

Evolution – The biological change in species. In Darwin's terms: 'descent by modification'.

Flake – A piece of stone, or flake, struck from a core.

Fossil – A relic or trace of former living organisms left in rock-formations.

Gene – A protein particle, forming part of a chromosome, by means of which hereditary characters are transmitted.

Glacial period – A time span encompassed by any one of the four major glacial advances of the Pleistocene.

Gravetian – Upper Palaeolithic tradition of Europe, extending from Russia to Spain and lasting from c. 27,000 B.C. to c. 19,000 B.C.

Hand-axe – An almond shaped stone implement mostly of flint or quartzite, symmetrical both bilaterally and bifacially and retouched on both borders.

Hominids – The family of man, including all species of Australopithecus and Homo.

Homo species – In their succession: Homo habilis, Homo erectus, Homo sapiens. (Homo sapiens neanderthalensis is now considered a sub-species of H. sapiens.) For more details consult the text: i.e., illustrations on sheet – one (brain and cultural curves, pp. 78-79.)

Hybrid – The offspring of the union of two distinct species.

Intelligence – Mental brightness, a person's degree of knowledge.

Kenyapithecus – Same as Ramapithecus.

Knapper – A stone tool maker.

Lamarckism – The theory of heredity which proclaims that characteristics acquired during a life-time, or by the greater use or disuse of organs, are inheritable.

Levalloisian-tools – A primitive hand-axe; forerunner of the Acheulian type.

Lingula – A small, bottom dwelling shellfish – an early living form surviving into the present age (*Phylum Brachiopoda*).

Littoral – Inhabiting the sea-shore.

Lobe – A division of the brain

frontal lobe: Controls movement

back or occipital lobe: Controls vision and emotion

parietal lobe: Controls and integrates sensory input.

Locus – A particular position in a particular chromosome.

Magdalenian – Upper Palaeolithic tradition, mainly in Europe from c. 16,000 B.C. to c. 10,000 B.C.

Mammalia – The highest class of animals producing living young and feeding them milk by means of their teats.

Melanin – A genetically linked granular pigment in human and animal tissue, causing a dark skin complexion.

Mesolithic – The pre-agricultural cultural period from c. 10,000 to 8000 B.C. in the Old World.

Microlith – A small stone artefact, normally under 3 cm. used for arrow tips and sickle blades.

Mousterian – A Middle Palaeolithic cultural assemblage mainly attributable to Neanderthal man.

Mutation – Sudden change or variation in the genetic equipment of a germ cell.

Neanderthalers (Neanders) – Homo sapiens Neanderthalensis (see under Homo-species).

Neolithic (New Stone Age) – First appearance of polished stone tools. Mainly associated with the advent of agriculture and stock-rearing.

Neo-Darwinism – Darwinism minus Lamarckian heredity. Lamarckism became obsolete with the advent of genetics.

Neo-Lamarckism – Attempts to revive a Lamarckian type inheritance.

Neurology – The study of nerves.

Obstetric limitation – The anatomical limits in the size of the woman's birth-channel.

Oldowan – Adjective form of 'Olduvai', applied to the early pebble-tools, of south and east Africa, originally found at Olduvai Gorge in N.Tanzania.

Olduvai Gorge – in N. Tanzania, famous for its extensive deposits of early human fossils and stone tools.

Osteodentokeratic – A term coined by Raymond Dart of an early hominid culture at Mapakansgate, South Africa, using bones for tools.

Palaeolithic – Old Stone Age, variously estimated – began 2.3 million years ago and finished c. 8000 B.C. (the beginning of the Neolithic).

Palaeo-Neurology – A study of the early structure of the nervous system.

Pebble tool – A crude tool made by breaking or splitting a water rounded pebble.

Phylogeny – History or development of a species, or race.

Pithecanthropus (Java man) – A Homo erectus fossil found in Java without stone tool connections.

Pleistocene – Sixth subdivision of the Cenozoic era. Estimated to reach back over a million years, up to 8000 years ago.

Polished stone axe – A form of stone axe, mostly made for hafting, produced by pecking, grinding and polishing. Estimated to have only appeared since the beginning of the Neolithic period.

Post-natal – Referring to the time just after a baby's birth.

Pressure flaking – Retouching flint implements by pressing the edge with a piece of wood or bone, instead of striking blows.

Primates – Include man, the apes, Old and New World monkeys, lemurs and tarsiers.

Punctational Evolution – In contrast to a slow and gradual process, a more explosive form of evolutionary change.

Quern – A hollowed stone for grinding cereals.

Reticulate Evolution – Results from a network-like mating of different races within the same species.

Retouching – The process of sharpening flint implements by the removal of small chips.

Scraper – Class of stone tools with retouch along one or more edges.

Sinanthropus (Peking man) – A race of H. erectus whose remains were found in Choukoutien near Peking.

Speciation – A division into different species.

Steinheim (female) – A Homo sapiens skull, c. 150,000 years old found near Steinheim, Germany.

Swanscombe fossil – A fragmentary female H. sapiens skull, of c. 200,000 B.P. found in England.

Taxa – A specific class of living organism.

Taxonomy – Science of the classification of living organisms and their sub-divisions.

Tertiary – Same as Cenozoic. The geological period from c.70 million years ago to the present.

Twa-Mbuti (Pygmies) – The type of aborigine inhabiting the Ituri Forest of the Congo.

Zinanthropus – Same as Australopithecus boisei.

PREFACE

Recent research has shown that Africa is the primeval fountain-head of hominid biological and cultural development. It endorses the contention of Cheikh Anta Diop and others that all human races past and present are descended from an originally dark-skinned African root-stock.

As for culture,[1] for many decades Cultural Anthropology has been dominated by the doctrine of cultural evolution. A re-assessment of hominid biological evolution and a re-evaluation of hunter-gatherer studies, demonstrate that this concept is no longer valid. Instead of a regular cultural evolutionary process we find an irregular medley of cultural events spanning the ages, wherein world-wide cultural parallels can mostly be related to common origins. Overall, this new cultural interpretation resembles in substance, though not in process, Darwin's idea on the origin of species, (insofar as the origin and spread of cultural elements is concerned), though in contrast to Darwin's ideas on biological evolution cultural relationships can not be related to biological evolutionary factors.

Based on such considerations the present treatise offers a long overdue critique of deeply-entrenched ideas in cultural and social anthropology.

The main themes are explored in four parts set out in two volumes. Volume One contains: Hominid Evolution and Cultural History, and: A Scrutiny of Cultural Theories. Volume Two to follow, contains: The Significance of Cultural Parallels, and: Speculating about the Origin of Civilization.

Part I

HOMINID EVOLUTION AND CULTURAL HISTORY

1. THE FOSSIL RECORD

I believe that human cultural events (human cultural history) can best be evaluated if placed against the background of human biological evolution. A first step in this direction is an investigation of the fossil record.

Commenting on this rise of the human species from some ape-like ancestor, Professor P.V. Tobias, one of the world's leading authorities on hominid evolution and brain development (1983b) has cited evidence suggesting that Modern Man and the Modern African great apes (chimpanzee and gorilla) are quite closely related genetically; so closely indeed, that much more recent divergence of the hominid lineage from the African apes seems to be the only possible explanation. Also of interest, the genetic distance between man, chimpanzee and gorilla was found to be far smaller than that between any of these and the great Asian ape, the orang-utan. For instance, the chimpanzee is far closer to man than to the orang-utang, not perceived in earlier studies.

Opinions about the further evolution of the genus hominidae remain volatile. Ever since hominid fossils were found and described (or dismissed as non-hominid) controversy has raged about the correct succession of hominid descent. It took Professor Raymond Dart's Taung Baby: Australopithecus (A.) africanus several decades to be confirmed as a genuine hominid. Meanwhile disputes about the exact succession of hominid species have involved such types as A. boisei, A. afarensis, A. robustus, Homo habilis, H. erectus, and H. neanderthalensis. Formerly it was thought that all of these may have had a common ancestor, the pre-hominid Ramapithecus (R.), bearing in mind that there is a large gap in existing fossil evidence between R. and the earliest A. (i.e., of between c. 8 million years and 3.75 million years – Pilebeam: 1960). This theory has now been abandoned with new discoveries of more complete specimens of R. and a revaluation of their morphology, indicating that R. may after all be in the orang-utan line, which split off from the African hominid lineage, between c. 16 million years and 10 million years B.P. (Tobias, 1983 b).

More recent research proposes drastic adjustments in the fossil record concerning both Neanderthalers and Modern Homo sapiens. Hitherto one theory had been that Homo sapiens evolved from the Neanderthalers who emerged c. 75,000 years ago in the evolutionary time scale. At that stage Cro-Magnon, the Modern type of Homo sapiens were presumed to have appeared c. 40,000 years ago. Now the Neanderthalers have been reassigned a time sequence of between 150,000 and 30,000 years B.P. (Gowlett, 1986), being classified as Homo sapiens neanderthalensis. Moreover the emergence of the Modern Homo sapiens is now put at between 100,000 and 120,000 years ago, while what is called the more archaic type of Homo sapiens reaches back to between 300,000 and 400,000 years (having arisen from Homo erectus stock).

In an article entitled 'Africa: Cradle of Modern Humans' (Science; 11.9.1987, pp 1292–95) R. Lewis proposes that all Modern Humans derive from a population that lived 200,000 years ago in Africa from where some of them migrated to the rest of the Old World about 100,000 years later.

Professor Tobias comments (personal communication, 1988) that the first suggestion of anatomically modern Homo sapiens with a probable date of 100,000 years comes from the Border Cave situated between Kwa Zulu and Swaziland. Another South African find with a maximum early date of 120,000 years B.P. comes from the Klasies River Mouth Cave in the Cape Province, where investigators found anatomically modern Homo sapiens skeletal remains. 'I am not sure' writes Tobias, 'where Roger Lewin gets the information about 200,000 years ago?'[1]

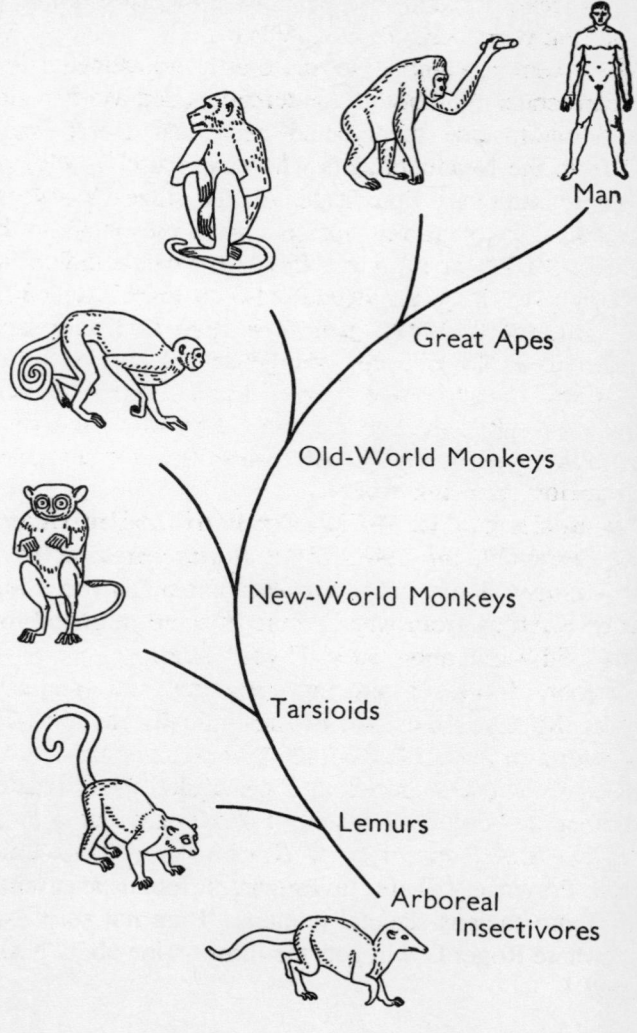

Man

Great Apes

Old-World Monkeys

New-World Monkeys

Tarsioids

Lemurs

Arboreal
Insectivores

Figure 1. The family tree of the primates. These represent the main groups of the primates.

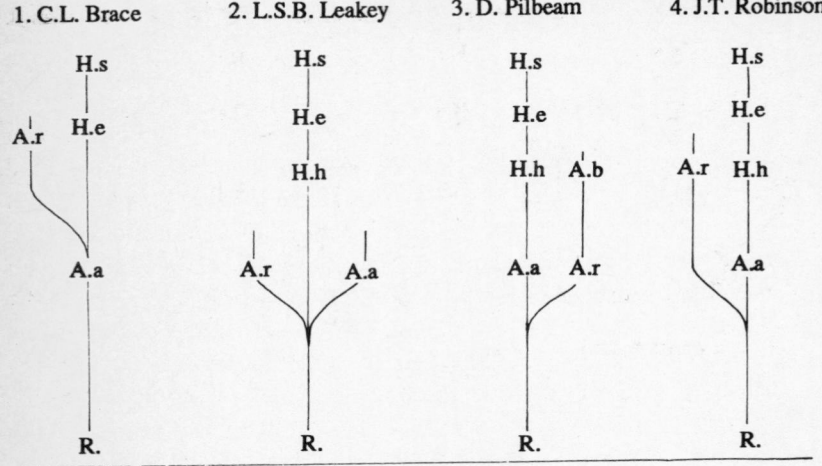

Figure 2. Diagrams illustrating differences of opinion on the succession of hominid descent.

Please note: The distances plotted are in no relation to chronology

Explanatory Notes:
R.   =   Ramapithecus
R.p =   Ramapithecus punjabicus
K.   =   Kenyapithecus (same as R.p)
A.af =   Australopithecus afarensis
A.a =   Australopithecus africanus
A.r =   Australopithecus robustus (formerly Paranthropus)
A.b =   Australopithecus boisei (formerly Zinjanthropus boisei)

H.h =   Homo habilis
H.e =   Homo erectus
H.s =   Homo sapiens

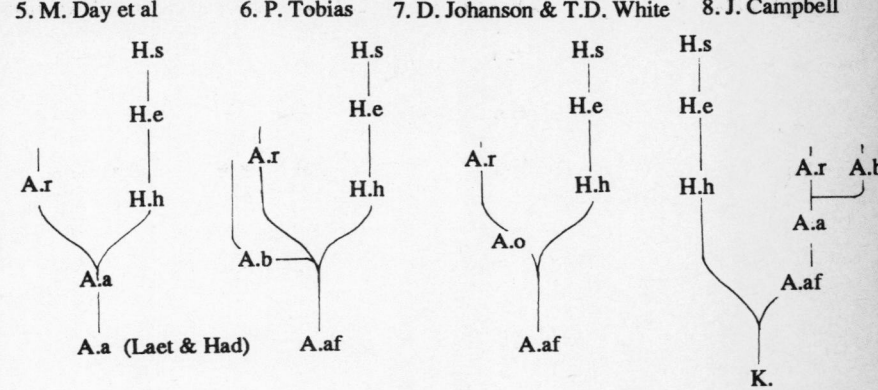

5. M. Day et al   6. P. Tobias   7. D. Johanson & T.D. White   8. J. Campbell

1.) C.L. Brace presents one continuous line of descent with A.af being included in A.a (from 'Lucy' 1981).

2.) L.S.B. Leakey assumes a common ancestor R., leading straight on to H.h. with an early separation of both, A.r and A.a.

3.) D. Pilbeam projects a direct line from R. to A.a etc, with a side branch incorporating both, A.r and A.b.

4.) J.T. Robinson offers the same as 3.) except that the branch-off accommodates only A.r (quotes 2.), 3.), 4.)) from Encyclop. of Anthropology, 1976.

5.) M. Day et al, does not recognize A.af, which he considers part of the single species A.a; with A.r branching-off separately.

6.) P.V. Tobias treats A.a as the rootstock of all other subsequent hominids; allocates A.r & A.b to separate branches (1983a).

7.) D. Johanson and T.D. White, treat A.af as the rootstock of all other hominids, allocates A.a and A.r to a separate branch.

8.) J. Campbell, (1983), projects K. as a common ancestor, leading directly to H.h, etc; with a separate branch accommodating A.af, A.a, A.r, and A.b.

7

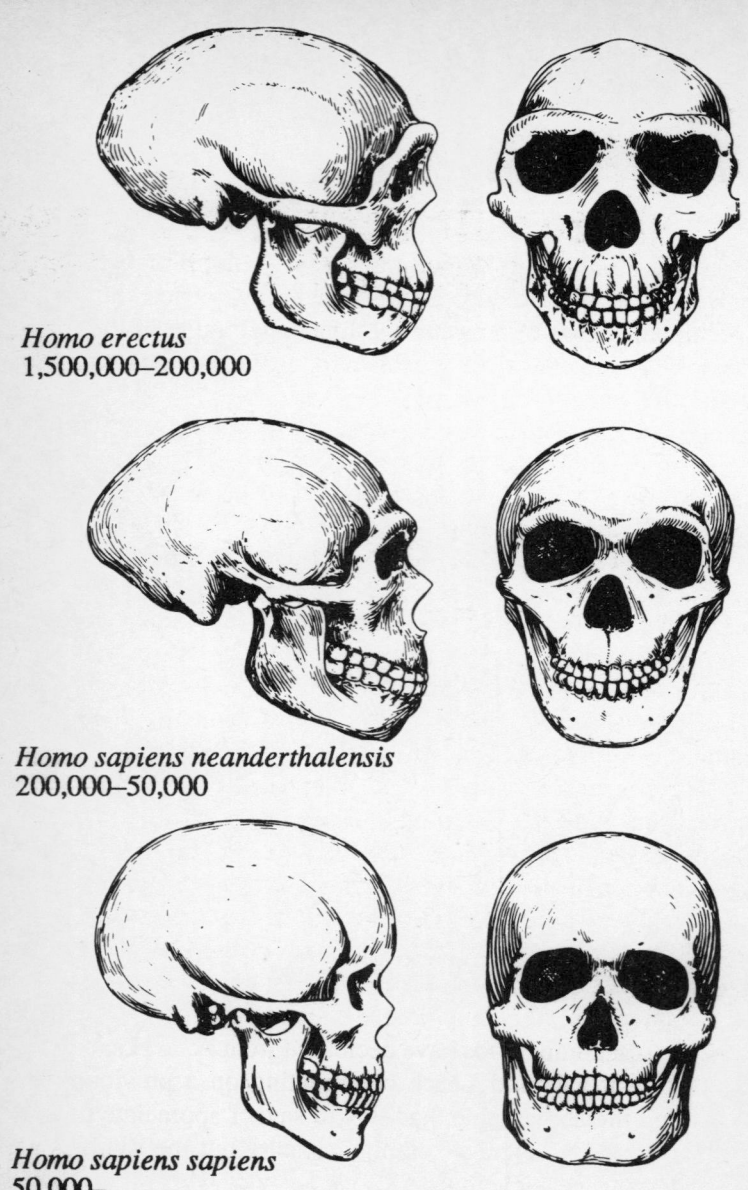

Homo erectus
1,500,000–200,000

Homo sapiens neanderthalensis
200,000–50,000

Homo sapiens sapiens
50,000–

Figure 3. Skulls illustrating the evolution in shape of humankind from the earliest time to the present.

2. BRAIN EVOLUTION IN GENERAL

Present assessments of hominid brain evolution must necessarily be based on brain size only, since no valid denominator exists to measure the functional value of the brain. Neither is there any discoverable link between brain size and intellectual potential, though, as will be hinted later, a certain marginal relationship seems to exist.

Dean Falk (1980), has pointed out that it is largely through R.L. Holloway's efforts that we know that brain size increased from c.450 cc in the Australopithecines (A.), to c.1400 cc in modern humans, and that hominid brain size has more than tripled since the time of A. (Holloway, 1975). As to the relationship between brain size and body size, Holloway and Post (1980), correctly point out that relative brain size has increased steadily from A. to H. sapiens (H.s.)

'Brain size in H.s. is c.3.1 times that predicted for nonhuman primates of equivalent body size (Passigham 1975)'.

'Further, indices show that man's neocortex is c. 3 times as large as that expected for a non-human primate of the same body size. It appears', continues Falk, 'that encephalization at birth is not higher in humans than in non-human primates ... the postponement of three-quarters of brain-growth in humans to postnatal periods should be viewed in terms of obstetrical limitations. Hence, to pass through the pelvic canal, a human neonate must be born at a more immature (more altricial) stage. Accordingly newborn/adult brain ratios have decreased from A. to H.s.'

Professor Edmund Leach commenting on a previous draft containing the above table, had this to say: 'I appreciate that the chart is based on 'average' cranial capacity but the samples are so small as to be meaningless'. This point has been duly taken into account in a separate treatise by Tobias (1983 a; pp 101–103). Remarking on the number of Early Hominid individuals recovered from African sites over 3 million years, Tobias admits

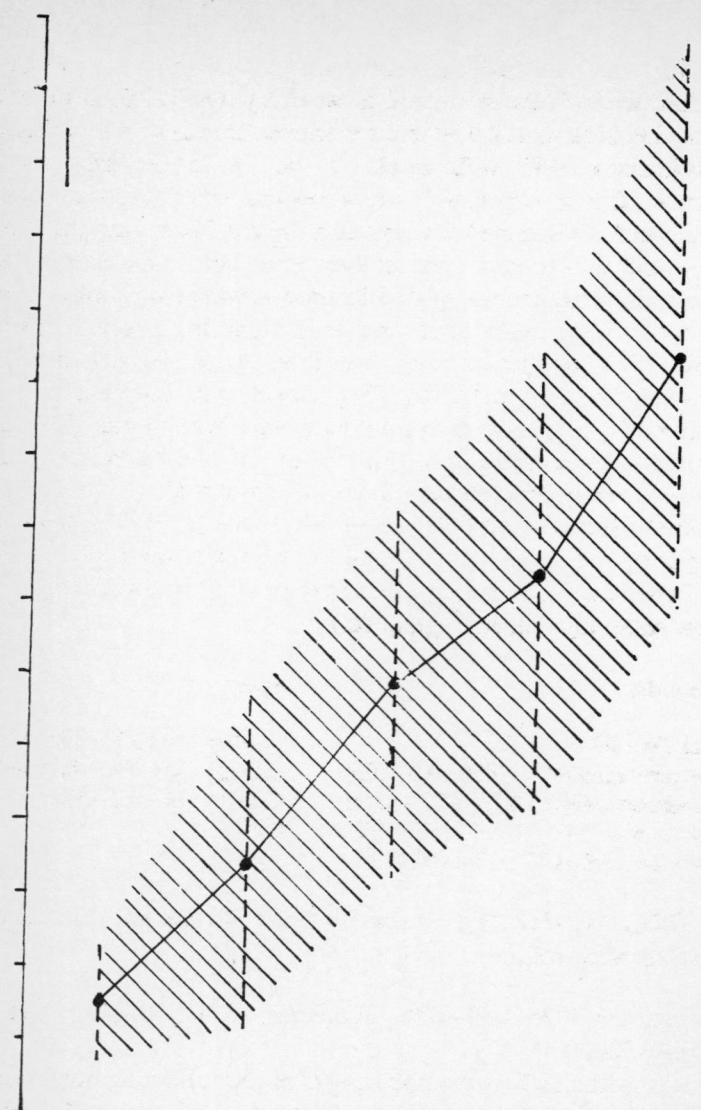

Figure 4. Mean cranial capacity and 95% population limits for five taxa of hominids to show the trebling in capacity between A. africanus and present-day H. sapiens.
The above table prepared by P.V. Tobias (who is a close collaborator of Professor Holloway), gives an up to date picture of average cranial capacities for the five taxa of hominids (1982).

that when the data so far collected are broken down the number of fossil individuals recovered is woefully small. 'To a human population biologist, for whom the sample size is often a critical consideration, 485 individuals is not a particularly large example. This is especially true when one considers that these 485 individuals spanned not less than three million years, that is, from about four to about one million years before the present. If our fossils were evenly spaced in time – which of course they are not – we should have one individual for every 6185$\frac{1}{2}$ years.' P.V. Tobias concludes that 'Despite the shortcomings of the fossil hominid data, the almost explosive increase in the number of specimen in the past quarter of a century has given us a much clearer picture of the nature of the morphological hominids and of the pattern of hominid evolution'.

Past figures compiled by Prof. Michael Day (1973) show in comparison to P.V. Tobias' table that cranial assessments of hominids have little changed during the past decades (the figures below state: low–mean–high in cc.)

Hominids:

H.habilis 510–639–770
Pithecantropus (H.e.) 700–880–1060
Sinanthropus (H.e.) 845–1057–1305
Modern man (H.s.) 1070–1370–1670
Australopithecus 405–500–605

Apes:

Chimpanzee 320–395–410
Orang-utang 330–410–499
Gorilla 410–505–605

Other past figures given by Prof. Bernhard Campbell, (1974) read as follows:

A.africanus: 435–588–815; H.erectus 774–950–1225; H.s. 1000–1330–2000
B. Campbell also lists the *age-ranges* of the following hominids: (The two sets of figures show, 1. the *known age*, and 2. the *assumed age*)
Australopithecines: 5.5 million years/3 million years and 6 million years/1.3 million years
A. boisei: 3 million years/1.2 million years and 6 million years/1 million years

11

A.africanus (China–Kwangwangling–Calotte) c. 1.9 million years
A.africanus (Java–Sangiran) c. 1.9 million years

It should be noted that the presence of A. in Asia is still a matter of dispute (*see* J.L. Franzen, Dart Symposium, 1985).

P.V. Tobias (1982) suggests a span of 5 million years in which an ape-like ancestor to Australopithecus became converted to modern man. At an average generation length of c. 15 years, the following hominizing trends would have become established.

Uprightness in c. 100,000 generations (1.5 million years), with further perfecting requiring another more than c. 100,000 generations. *Change in teeth* 100,000 generations before reaching a hominid pattern and altogether 300,000 generations (4.5 million years) to reach the modern human pattern. *Brain enlargement* was not strikingly manifest for the first 100,000 generations and marked brain enlargement started late, at the stage of H. habilis, from c. 2.3 million years to 0.1 million years B.P., i.e. in just under 150,000 generations.

Evidence further suggests that brain enlargement was one of the last hominizing trends, but modern human proportions were then reached in a relatively small number of generations.

The following table prepared by P.V. Tobias (1986) gives a useful summary of evolutionary trends from the ape-line to H. sapiens, under the heading:

'Some suggested climacteric events in Hominid Evolution.'

Event:	*Possible/Approx. dating (Million years B.P.):*
1. Orang-utang divergence	16–10
2. Gorilla divergence	10–7 ?
3. Hominid-chimpanzee divergence	9–5 ?
4. Homo – A. divergence	2.3 (H.h. GK)
5. Earliest stone cultural remains	2.5–2.0
6. Acquisition of speech	2.0–1.5
7. Movements of hominids from Africa to Asia	1.8–1.5
8. H.h. – H.e. transition	1.6–1.5

SOME BASIC BRAIN FUNCTIONS

R.L. Holloway (1978, 1979) – quoted by R. Leakey, (1981) gives the following simplified summary:

The Brain is divided into four parts, or lobes. The frontal lobe controls movement, the back or occipital lobe vision and emotions, the side or temporal lobe, memory; above the temporal is the parietal lobe having the crucial role of comparing and integrating information that flows in through the sensory channels of vision, hearing, smell and touch. Roughly speaking, in the human brain the parietal and temporal lobes predominate, whereas in ape brains these areas are smaller.

Speech abilities are located in the Wernicke area, but the actual muscular movements for sound are located in the Broca area. Thus anatomically, the left hemisphere is rather larger than the right, and there is a detectable lump over the region that houses the Broca area. In apes the swelling is less pronounced.

R. Holloway further reminds us (quoted by R. Leakey, 1981) that the area which controls the fine action of the hands and the area governing muscular movements required for speech delivery lie very close – this may reflect shared origins.

Stressing the particular importance of the brain's asymmetry, P.V. Tobias (personal communication, 1987) explains that there is some evidence of the appearance of a degree of asymmetry in the brains of non-human primates, but it is widely believed that the asymmetries of structure and function have become more marked in the evolution of the hominids. 'My own studies on endocranial casts,' says Tobias, 'have attempted to cope with this problem, although our material remains very inadequate'.

So while brain size was increasing over the last two million years, very likely the degree of asymmetry was increasing; 'You could regard that as change in quality closer to the modern human brain'.

'Perhaps even more importantly, from about the stage of Homo habilis, according to my own heretical proposal of 1980 and now supported by several colleagues, the speech areas of the cerebral hemisphere have long been operative. Whilst poorly developed or absent in *Australopithecus africanus*, these "bumps" are very evident in Homo habilis and, coupled with other evidence of his cultural prowess they have led me to propose that speech, spoken language, didn't begin with the later forms of man, such as Neandertal or *Homo erectus*, but actually began before the end of the Tertiary in *Homo habilis* about two million years ago! ...

'I believe,' says P.V. Tobias, 'that the appearance of the faculty of language represents a qualitative change in the evolution of the hominid brain of enormous proportions. It is not merely an increase in the brain quality: it is a dramatic and revolutionary step forward, perhaps the most important single attainment in the entire history of the human species. I have called this moment of breakthrough, a revolution in hominid evolution.

'If the faculty of spoken language greatly enhanced group cohesion in primitive societies, if it helped to ensure the survival of a group (rather than of individuals), it could have been of very great selective importance and natural selection would certainly have favoured its development.'

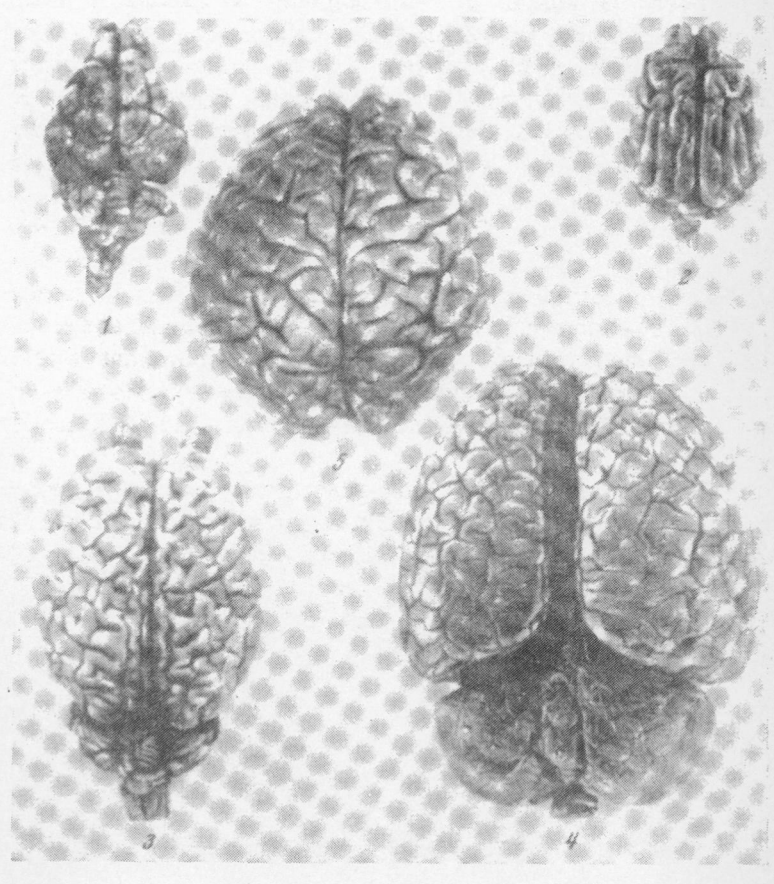

Figure 5. Human and mammal brains: 1 - kangaroo; 2 - dog; 3 - horse; 4 - elephant; 5 - man.

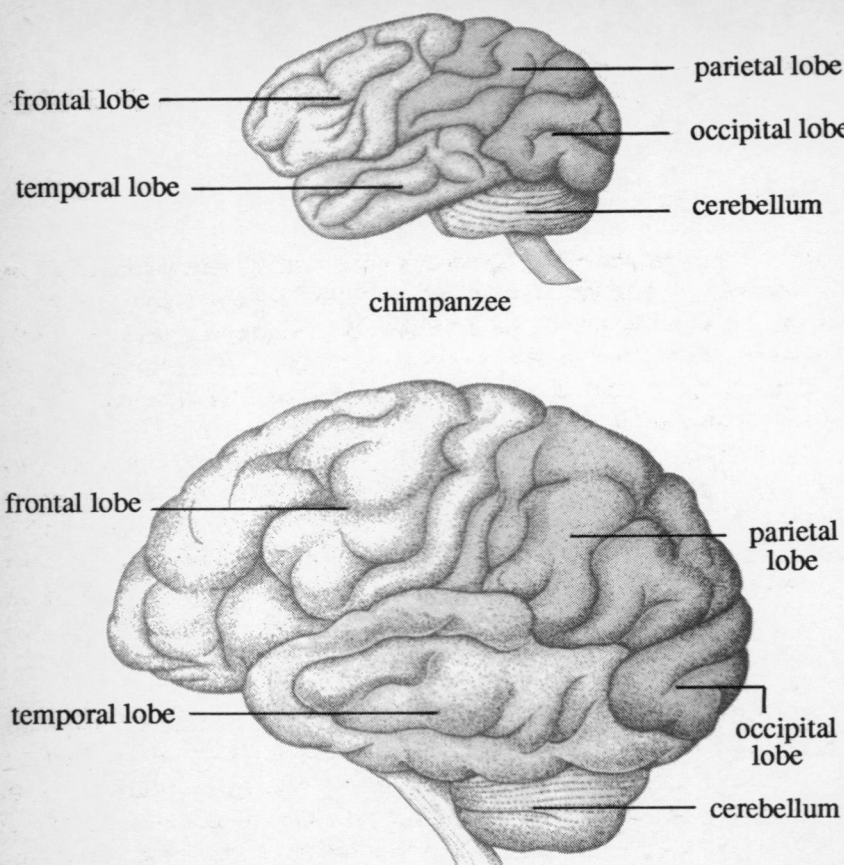

frontal lobe

parietal lobe

occipital lobe

temporal lobe

cerebellum

chimpanzee

frontal lobe

parietal lobe

temporal lobe

occipital lobe

cerebellum

human

Figure 6. The austrolopithecines' brains were not much larger than those of apes, but with the emergence of the Homo line there was a steady increase in the size of the brain. The shape of a human brain differs substantially from that of a chimpanzee, with certain brain lobes becoming increasingly dominant. These are the temporal lobe, responsible for memory, and the parietal lobe which integrates information received from the senses. This change in shape is evident at a very early stage in hominid evolution, and, surprisingly, even the small-brained austrolopithecines had a basically human brain form.
From R. Leakey: ***The Making of Man*** **(1981).**

3. BRAIN SIZE IN GENERAL

Various authorities have commented on the relationship of brain-size and intelligence. Johanson (1982) has remarked '... that the differences in brain size within our species appear to have no significant correlation with the intelligence of their owners. Rather they reflect differences in body-size. Big men have big brains, but they are no smarter than small men. Men are also larger than women and have consistently larger brains, but the two sexes are of equal intelligence. Since there has always been a high degree of sexual dimorphism in hominids, it must be accepted there will be size differences in fossil skulls. If a large and a small skull are alike in every respect but size, the possibility cannot be ignored that the small one may be a female and the large one a male – and that they are the same species despite size difference'.

A study of brain sizes carried out by G. von Bonin (1963) led him to conclude that there was no apparent correlation between the average cranial capacity and the cultural status of the various races. Generally, the weight of the brain is a poor indicator of its functional value. Moreover, G. von Bonin pointed out, in any major series of skulls, the capacity will vary between say, 1800 and 1200 cc., without any apparent corresponding correlation with function. Still it has been said that a certain amount of brain is necessary for normal function of the individual. Keith (1948) has spoken of a cerebral Rubicon which he put at 800 cc; only when the cranial capacity is greater than this amount are we justified in assuming a human intelligence and that ability to learn which appears necessary for human status.

R. Dart (1956) has disputed such arbitrary limitations by citing examples of Bantus with a capacity of 511 cc., 519 cc., and 560 cc., who functioned normally as herdboys and farmhands. 'A Bantu woman with only 340 cc., was able to do some routine work and could dance when she heard music.' Other examples by G. von Bonin are of people within between 340 and 490 cc. 'Some of these are marked as "idiots". But the fact is, that most people have much greater brain weight and that the average is about 1400 cc.'

On the other end of the scale we get the recorded brain sizes of Cromwell and Lord Byron of 2350 cc. (Dart, 1956). Pearson (1925) showed that some very gifted persons including Leon Gambetta, Anatole France and Franz Josph Gall, had small brains of about 1100 grams, while Dr. Johnson's was over 2000 grams. He concluded that correlation between brain size and mental capacity was not significant.

Similar ideas have lately been voiced by Johanson. He writes (1982): 'Brain size alone is now recognized as a questionable index of species identification because of its variability. People today have brains that range in size between 1000 and 1800 cc. and in their lower range actually overlap the brains of H. erectus, which run from 700 to 1250 cc. If the largest brained H. erectus were to be rated against the smallest brained sapiens – and all their other attributes ignored – their species names would have to be reversed. Similarly, the habilis brain overlaps that of erectus, varying between 500 and 800 cc.'

All this does not alter the fact that within the four million years of hominid evolution under review (from A. afarensis to Homo sapiens) there has been an increase in average brain size of about 1000 cc. (from c. 415 to c. 1350 cc.). While we therefore cannot say that increase in brain size is directly responsible for cultural progress we ought to allow it at least a marginal influence.

From all the preceding details it appears that, although in recent times a reasonable consensus has emerged, both in respect of the ages of the different hominid species, their succession and their brain sizes, the situation remains still too volatile to establish a reliable lineage of hominid descent. When I therefore submit the diagram of a brain-curve later in the text, it must be considered provisional and symbolic only, and subject to adjustments in the light of future new fossil discoveries.

THE ANTIQUITY AND BRAIN SIZE OF HOMO SAPIENS

Concerning the brain of homo sapiens some remarkable facts can be noted. They show that during the last decades his age estimate has expanded beyond any foreseeable bounds, while in contrast, his average brain assessment has decreased.

For example, only a few decades ago, the age of homo sapiens was put at not more than 10,000 years, and as recently as the late 1960s (noted while researching for my book, *Homo Sapiens in Decline* (1973), H.s. age estimate ranged between 60,000 and 35,000 years B.P. Charlton Coon (1967), put H.s. age at 35,000; and the same figure is given by Bray/Trump (1970). Only a few years later, Bernhard Campbell (1974), advanced H.s. age to between 300,000 and 250,000 B.P. While Johanson (1982) put H.s. beginnings at between 500,000 B.P. and 200,000 B.P. Finally, Joseph Campbell (1983) has referred to a fossil find at Vertescollos Hungary, which he describes as Homo sapiens, with an age tag of half a million years (this has since been corrected to c. 200,000 years).

As to homo sapiens brain size, W.W. Howells (1967) suggested an average value of 1450 cc, while G.v. Bonin (1963), lists 1400 cc. In comparison, more recent figures put the mean brain size of H.s. at 1370 cc. (M. Day, 1973:90), 1330 cc. (B. Campbell, 1974), 1300 cc. (Enzycl. of Anthrop. 1976), and 1345 cc., (P.V. Tobias, 1983a).

What is also remarkable about H.s. brain size is, that during the Upper Palaeolithic H.s. showed bigger average brain sizes than contemporary humans. For example, G.v. Bonin (1963) wrote that the skull capacity of the Upper Palaeolithics is greater than almost all modern races by 40 cc. to 50 cc. A still greater discrepancy has been observed between the mean brain size of modern man and the classical Neanderthalers by M. Day (1973), the comparative figures being 1470 against 1370 – a difference of 100 cc.; Howells and Trinkaus (1980) speak of a mean for Neanders, of 1600 cc.

M. Day (1973), also quotes Thomas (1969), who stresses the shrinking of cranial capacities in recent man. Thomas estimates the male brain capacity of the Upper Palaeolithics at c. 1600 cc., adding that this amounts to a mean of 1520 cc. for the two sizes taken together. He remarks that 'Since present cranial capacity is about 1350 cc. throughout the world (personal mean: 1971), there has been thus more than 10% reduction, bearing on volume and not on functional value'.

4. THE USE OF TOOLS AND ARTEFACTS

The archaeological record of stone-tools through the ages has been habitually used as a yardstick to measure cultural progress, at least up to the Neander–Mousterian sequence (put by J. Gowlett 1984, at c. 150,000 years B.P.) On the other hand early man's cultural achievements are enhanced by such feats as the possible use of stone-walling for shelters, the sharing of food, etc., dating back two million years (P.V. Tobias, 1983a), as well as the use and making of fire dating to c. 1.7 million years ago (Gowlett, 1984). All of these hint at early man's intellectual potentials. Yet such and other cultural indicators are of much too sporadic a nature to serve as comparative cultural parameters.

On the other hand, there can be little doubt that even the most primitive of hominids, in all likelihood, used wood, plain stones of all sizes and shapes, bone and other materials for tools and weapons before making and using stone tools. G.M. Guilmet in an interesting study (MAN, April 1977) observes: 'Hominids most likely made their first tools from wood, grass or bone with the aid of their teeth or fingers. This behaviour would be analogous to that of the chimpanzee. Artefacts made from such perishable materials would probably not appear in the archaeological record and would be hard to distinguish from naturally modified objects (Oakley 1972)'. It is therefore only by analogy that this point can be proved.

Studies of living non-human primates give definite proof of tool use (mainly wood). Numerous examples of this are recorded by G.M. Guilmet (MAN, April 1977). He mentions Goodall (1964) who observed Chimpanzees in the wild throwing objects at their own kind, at Baboons and at humans, particularly in aggressive situations. Gorillas and Orang utangs using dislodged branches to rake fruit; Colobus, Mangabeys and Baboons using sticks to stir up insects hidden under stones; Chimpanzees using stalks, stems and twigs to probe for termites and to collect honey from beehives. Goodall (1964) also observed that tool-making and tool-using skills as a kind of cultural tradition were passed on by Chimpanzees from one generation to the next in the Gombe Stream area. According to Richard Leakey and R. Levin (1981), Chimps and Gorillas are adept weavers, both making sleeping nests for themselves by threading branches, twigs and leaves.

It may be suggested that hominids, upon reaching a certain brain capacity, used spears, possibly of hardwood,[1] and also loose stones and even bolas[2] as missiles, to defend themselves against predators and to hunt animals.. They may also have used wooden implements and tools for all kinds of camp-site chores, long before making stone-tools.

One implement of great age with global significance is the 'metate', a stone slab used for grinding seeds by means of the 'mano' or grinding implement. The merit of having rescued it from oblivion must go to George Carter, who has described it at length in 'The Metate: An Early Grain Grinding Implement in the New World' (1973), and other papers. He writes that these (Metate and Mano), go back through the Mousterian Period in Africa. Its world wide continuous distribution stretches as far as Australia, and the Americas. It appears in the alluvial covers on the interglacial beaches in Southern California, 120,000 years ago. The conclusion is that although most of mankind had the metate for grinding seeds (and possibly ochre as well), for hundreds of thousands of years, it is almost certain that only in one place (c.10,000 years ago), as a further development the actual cultivation of cereals may have begun.

According to J.C. Campbell, (1983), 'there is convincing

Figure 7. Chimpanzee mother and young use sticks for collecting ants to eat.
From R. Leakey, R. Lewin: *People of the Lake* **(1979).**

evidence at this early age of the use of weapons to kill game, but it is quite possible that sticks and bones would have been used as clubs (Wolberg, 1970). Sticks are shown in antagonistic display by apes (Hall, 1963a) and would almost certainly have been used as clubs by hominids. Also, techniques of killing must have been developed that did not involve the use of sharp canine teeth.

A more comprehensive argument in this respect was put forward by Dart (1957) when he advanced the hotly disputed Osteodentokeratic Culture of A. africanus, located at Mapakansgate, South Africa. Dart argued that A. africanus utilized the skeletal remains of animals as tools. Bone, teeth and horns, served for daggers, picks, digging sticks, chisels, scoops, gauges, bowls, cups and other tools and weapons. With some of these, Dart maintained, the Australopithecines, particularly A. Africanus, must have hunted baboons, fellow Australopithecines, and other creatures. See also Wolberg (1970) for a supportive and thorough review of Dart's work as well as the reaction to it by the scientific community.

P.V. Tobias informs me (personal communication, 1987) that it is held by many workers today that the newer work on alternative agencies for the accumulation of bones (at Mapakansgate), has largely laid Prof. Dart's concept at rest. He further tells me that he sees little evidence that Australopithecus (A.), as we know him from Sterkfontein and Mapakansgate, went beyond the stage of tool-using in perishable media (i.e., A. was not a stone-tool maker). Nevertheless as P.V. Tobias had pointed out before (1971), 'A. lived in a habitat providing little natural protection, and had no natural weapons of offence and defence and no threatening large canines – his very survival depended on implemental activities.'

The earliest stone tools so far claimed are those of A. afarensis from Gonda/Hadar, Ethopia. Johanson (1982), holds them to be the oldest tools known anywhere in the world, with an age estimate of c. $2\frac{1}{2}$ million years. Homo habilis from Olduvai Gorge seems to be the next oldest tool maker, and Mary Leakey has commented (1971), that their tool-making ability is now being generally accepted. In contrast, contemporary A.

boisei is adjudged a doubtful tool-maker. The age of the Oldowan tools of H. habilis is put at c. 2 million years.

Concerning the A. afarensis tools mentioned above, Johanson (1982), records that they were of basalt and of an actually better workmanship than the later Oldowan tools of H. habilis. 'They were a stunning surprise. And they tended to strengthen my published opinion that the large Hominids at Hadar were Homo.'

It is generally believed that bi-pedalism, leaving the hands free, promoted a more effective tool-shaping and tool-using capacity. Reciprocally, the increasingly more effective use of tools may have promoted bi-pedalism by means of natural selection.

This is not exactly the opinion of Owen Lovejoy, a locomotion expert. In a conversation recorded by Johanson (1982), he maintains that from the standpoint of pure efficiency, bi-pedalism is a preposterous way of running. Responds Johanson: 'Man was a tool user. He had to stand up in order to have his hands free to carry tools and weapons'. Lovejoy in response: 'Ultimately, yes. But originally, rubbish. That idea never did make sense. Now it is exploded by the Laetoli and Hadar fossils. They were walking that way maybe a million years before their descendants began using tools'.

In my opinion this is a weak argument because although there is no evidence that earliest A. afarensis made stone tools, he most likely used wooden tools and weapons and loose unworked stones, a million or more years beforehand.

This view is supported by R. Leakey (1981), who writes that even Chimpanzees occasionally use a stone to smash open hard nuts. He also suggests that the first stone tool technology was probably needed to fashion other tools of wood. This, says Leakey, could have gone on for millions of years while leaving absolutely no detectable trace. Such tools might be as old as 6 million years or even more and may lay scattered throughout ancient deposits in many parts of Africa.

Other factors which have been cited to explain evolutionary brain increases are the enlargement of the visual cortex and the use of articulate speech, serving to enlarge those parts of the brain which are concerned with speech and memory. Speech ought to have been of increasing importance for achieving better communication within the closely knit primitive family group, as well as in teaching growing infants. Another factor to be considered may have been the gradually growing need of greater childhood care, which in humans reaches up to age eight or ten, before infants can be presumed to become self-supporting adolescents. During the mother's and child's nursing period, the male members had to be the main providers.

Whatever the case, the fact is that average hominid brain sizes, over the last four million years increased by 1000 cc. Whether this increase has influenced cultural progress is a question which must remain unresolved for the present. As to stone tool improvement throughout the three million years of the palaeolithic, 'All that can be traced,' remarks Lia de Paor (1971), is 'the painfully slow improvement in technique of a few simple types'.

Similar views were voiced by Johanson (1982), who writes 'There are differences in workmanship that do say something about a tool's age. There is the extremely primitive Oldowan industry. Identified and named by the Leakeys at Olduvai Gorge and now known to date back at least 1.8 million years and probably 2 million years on the evidence of similar artifacts found at Omo and Lake Turkana. There is also the more advanced Acheulian industry, generally believed to be associated with Homo erectus. With both seeming to have appeared rather suddenly at about 1.5 million years ago, and to have evolved little thereafter, stubbornly resistant to change for at least a million years.[3] It would seem that the needs of the Early African hunter-gatherers were adequately served by the Acheulian tool kit and that there was little reason to improve on it'. According to J. Gowlett (1984), 'The older forms of core-tools, flakes and scrapers continue throughout the Acheulian, and on some sites they greatly outnumber the hand-axes'.

5. POST-ACHEULIAN CULTURES

Coming after the long, rather culturally stagnant, Acheulian sequence, the following is a condensed account of subsequent cultural developments, beginning with the Mousterian/Neanderthal phase. All of this is given graphical expression in the Cultural Curves D-II, D-IV and D-V.

A. THE NEANDERTHALERS.[4]

According to W.W. Howells and E. Trinkaus (1980): 'Antecedents that ally themselves closely with the Neanderthalers can now be found in the well known Swanscombe skull from England, the Fontechevade skull from France and the Steinheim skull from Germany' (all of them now classified under Homo sapiens–G.K.). Following the Acheulian, the Neanderthal/Mousterian phase, represents a considerable advance in stone tool technology. Clark/Piggott write (1970) 'Even the most perfectly finished hand-axe presented no more than the culmination of a process of refining a primitive chopper tool. In contrast, the production of complete implements at a single blow from cores previously prepared so as to ensure that the flakes when detached conformed to desired patterns, was something new. It was a Neanderthal achievement'.[1] The N.s also were the first humans known to have buried their dead, sprinkled them with red-ochre, and accompanied them with flint implements and animal remains.

They are also known to have used wooden spears for weapons, and animal pelts for clothing, although living in caves, they are reputed to have used skin-tents, when camping in the open (v. Bonin 1963).

Physically, the former view that they were ugly slouching brutes has been discarded. As already mentioned before, their average brain size was c.1600 cc, being significantly larger than that of modern humans. The Encyclopedia of Anthropology

1976, has listed Neanderthal remains in Belgium, W. Germany, France, Gibraltar, Zambia, S. Africa, Java, Uzbekistan, Iraq, Italy and Yugoslavia.

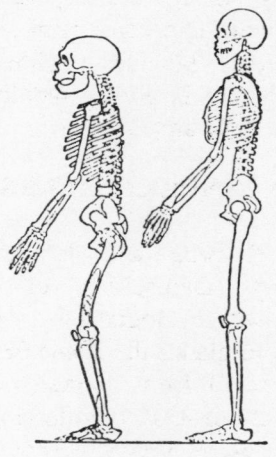

Figure 8. Comparison of the stance of Neanderthal (Homo sapiens) and Cromagnon man (Homo sapiens sapiens).

B. THE UPPER PALAEOLITHICS

They have been described as being physically much like modern humans, while culturally they can be divided into many groups, the principal ones being the Aurignacian–Gravettian (c.40,000–18,000 B.C.), and the Solutrean–Magdalenian (c.18,000–10,000 B.C.). Prominent among the U.P.s were the Cro–Magnons. According to Clark/Piggott (1970), they first emerged nearly 40,000 years ago among Neanderthal groups somewhere between the east Mediterranean and the mountains of inner Asia. Aurignacian cultural achievements include the production of a variety of artefacts of stone, fish-bone, and mammoth ivory, some still unsurpassed in their excellence. The first examples of cave-art are attributed to the Aurignacians of the west who also continued the use of red ochre (a specific Neanderthal innovation) at their much more elaborate burials. Their contemporaries, the Gravettians, were adept in producing figurines of animals and women, carved in ivory and other material, or baked in clay. One remarkable product of their genre were the so-called Venus figurines. Clark/Piggott contend that the spread of these figurines agrees closely with the dispersal of the Gravettian culture as a whole. Venus figurines are found over distances of 2000 miles (3200 km) ranging from the banks of the Don (s.e. Russia) to the foothills of the Pyrenees in Spain. 'The general resemblance of these figurines is so close as to suggest the movement of actual people – and this impression is heightened by the similarity in flint work, in decorative art, and in east and central Europe, in the display of Mammoth and cave-art'. Cave art again reached its height in the Magdalenian phase, experiencing a wide geographical spread. Clark/Piggott record that 'Cave-art in the Capora Cave in the southern Urals, is of a comparable style to that of the Dordogne in France, 2500 miles (over 4000 km) to the west.'

C. THE MESOLITHIC PHASE

This is generally considered the short transitory period between the end of the Palaeolithic (Old Stone Age), and the Neolithic (New Stone Age), although the latter denotation has not much to do with stones, but rather marks the beginnings of farming and stock rearing.

A typical Mesolithic example is the Natufian Culture of Palestine (c. 11,000 to 8,000 B.C.). There is a prevalence of basket remains, sickles, querns and grind-stones which indicate a pre-agricultural specialized, food-collecting phase. Similar patterns within the same time-context have been found at Zawi-Chami in N. Iran and at the Belt-Cave, south of the Caspian (8th millennium B.C.).

A similar pre-agricultural trend has been described by Willey (see Caldwell, 1962), in the so-called Desert Cultures of the North American southwest c. 8000–5000 B.C.

D. THE NEOLITHIC SEQUENCE
(c. 8000 TO c. 4000 B.C.)

Marks the advent of farming and stock-rearing, of pottery and the first appearance of fully ground and polished stone-axes.

As to agricultural beginnings, Mellaart (1967), among others, has shown that by 7000 B.C. wheat and barley growing was firmly established in three main areas of the Near East: Hacilar in Western Anatolia, Beidha in Jordan, and Ali Kosh in Khusistan. Based on traces of ancient irrigation works found in Highland New Guinea it has been conjectured that horticulture may have been practised there as early as 8000 B.C. (10,000 B.P.) or even earlier. The spread of wheat farming from the Near East to Europe has been plotted by R.A. Jairazbhoy (1982). His listings are: c. 6100 B.C. Crete (Knossos); c. 5820 B.C. Corfu (Sidari); c. 5550 B.C. Thessaly (Argisa); c. 5605 B.C. Italy (Calabria); c. 5570 B.C. France (Bouches de Rhone); c. 5353 B.C. Bulgaria (Karanova); c. 5140 B.C. Hungary (Gyalaret); c. 4915 B.C. Yugoslavia (Vrsnik); c. 4450 B.C. Czechoslovakia (Chabarovice); c. 3620 B.C. Poland (Sarnova); and c. 3415 B.C. Great Britain (Lambourne Berks).

Other important cultural firsts which can be placed within the time bracket of 10,000 B.C. and 4,000 B.C. (covering the Mesolithic and the Neolithic periods) are the following: pottery, textiles, basketry, the use of copper, obsidian, bitumen, use of mud-bricks, and construction of solid houses. As to fully ground and polished (hafted) stone-axes, the word fully needs emphasis, as edge ground – but not fully ground and polished stone axes of earlier date, have been recorded in an Australian orbit. (Arnhem–Land, age c. 23,000 B.C., and Huon–Peninsula, age c. 38,000 B.C.). These dates may however be questionable.

E. EARLY CIVILIZATIONS

This subject, as far as origins are concerned, is treated at length in PART III of the work. Here in PART I we are concerned only with the cultural achievements specific to the early civilizations. These are listed below and later plotted against the hominid curve of Diagram D-V. (See pp. 78-79.) All fit into the time bracket of between c. 4500 and c. 2500 B.C. One hurdle to be passed first, however, is to define the term civilization, which finds differing interpretations. Some prominent prehistorians, like Prof. Fred Wendorf, of the South Methodist University in Dallas, Texas, and others would rather avoid the term civilization altogether, and prefer to speak of 'Complex Societies'. (For more details see chapter eleven.)

Here we retain the term, though limiting it specifically to those earliest, as well as later civilizations, which can be described as 'Urban Literate'. Their prototypes are the civilizations of Egypt and Sumer which emerged almost simultaneously between c. 3300 B.C. and c. 3100 B.C. Both contain cultural elements of great likeness, in their details of material culture, and their ideational components. Other early civilizations differing only in detail, but not in substance, emerged subsequently in India, China, Mexico (including Mesoamerica) and Peru.

Their most distinctive and common feature is their agricultural background, which, in the Old World was based on big river irrigation (i.e., Nile, Tigris/Euphrates, Indus, Hoangho). They also show the first historical appearance of kings, both secular and divine, and in association with them the worship of gods in an organized religion. Other spectacular achievements in the Old World include monumental temple structures, pyramids and palaces and the emergence of large cities. They share the use of writing (though not evidenced universally) and the increased use of gold, precious or semi-precious stones and metals.

A summary of the principal cultural achievements over the last several million years, listed in the preceding account, is given in the Cultural Epoch chart (see pp.95-97), which divides humanity's cultural achievements into six broadly based historical epochs and contrasts them chronologically.

6. THE BRAIN'S INTELLECTUAL QUALITIES

A mong contemporary studies on this subject that of Dean Falk sums up the position admirably. He writes (1980): 'We pride ourselves that human intellectual achievements are so great that they must be the result of qualitative improvement in the human nervous system. According to this line of thought, it is not just that humans have more brains than did their early ancestors, but qualitatively better brains. But is this true? Various authors have racked the fossil record of hominid brains for an answer to this question.'

Below is my own effort to hint at a solution.

In my book, *Homo Sapiens in Decline* (1973), when commenting on 'The Role of Instincts', I wrote: 'The thesis of this book is that the motive of species preservation is the essence of all animal and human activities. In this process all biological properties have been developed by natural selection based on gene mutations. The living functions basic to this process were those of reflex-action, instinct, and reason.

'Instinctive urges are the primary forces that induce animals to act purposefully (i.e., keep alive and procreate). But such action requires the aid and guidance of the senses. Sensory perceptions and their interplay form the basis of the mental process, and involve, with the aid of memory, the capacity we call thinking or reasoning.' (For more details of my argument, see Appendix pp.97-101.)

The importance of the sensory input in brain evolution has been emphasized by G. von Bonin, a prominent American brain anatomist. In his book *The Evolution of the Human Brain*, he writes, (1963): 'One of the most important differences between higher and lower vertebrates that we are just beginning to appreciate is the much less variegated sensory input of the lower forms and the importance of this fact for the intelligence of the

31

animal. In this connection it should be particularly pointed out that one of the most important differences between primates and the other mammals is that the former rely more on vision than olfaction and, consequently, that the optic nerve gets much bigger and contains more fibres than in other forms. To cite but a few examples: dog and cat, about 150,000 fibres; pig and sheep about 600,000; and monkey and man, about 1,200,000. This means of course, that there is a much richer sensory input in primates than in other forms. Since it has been shown that the sensory input is necessary for a normal life of the cortex – at least in man – this may partly explain the greater intelligence of the primates, although it certainly is not the only factor.'

One may add that modern studies of the neurological structure of the brain have amply confirmed such developments. This applies particularly to the study of neuro-transmitters which transfer the electrical signals of the sensory impulses into chemical receptors, producing the desired physiological effects.

This point is further elucidated by P.V. Tobias (1971). He points out: 'An advancement of brain development has been proposed by Jerrison, producing interesting early confirmation of the rise in brain development of H. habilis over the Australopithecines. The results obtained, expressed in billions of neurons are:

African great apes 3.4 – 3.6	H. erectus 5.7 – 8.4
Australopithecines 3.9 – 4.5	H. sapiens (various
H. habilis 5.2 – 5.4	populations) 8.4 – 8.9.'

That there is however no definite correlation between brain size and brain quality has been emphasized by G. von Bonin (1963): ' ... the inside of the brain is sheathed in the "dura matter" and is seen as through a thick veil, so that very little can be discerned. It has been shown that the fissures of the human brain are quite variable and these variations do not appear to throw any light on the mental characteristics of the bearer.'

What about the other features of the brain? Certain scientists have based human brain superiority on the particular development of the frontal lobes. This view is rejected by v. Bonin, who believes that the importance of the frontal lobes has often been vastly exaggerated. Also, the more reliable indices show that the frontal lobes of hominoid fossil forms differ little in size from those of modern man, except that modern man's brains are generally larger. But in both types, the indices for the various parts of the brain do not differ greatly.

These views about human brain evolution, largely accepted on the authority of v. Bonin, are nowadays held by most brain anatomists.[1] It appears therefore that specific human brain qualities can neither be deduced from differences in brain volume nor from the shape of the brain itself. It is here that the factor of natural selection must be advanced. Its biological evolutionary significance is expressed in Julian Huxley's dictum: *'No evolutionary trend can be maintained except by natural selection'.* (1957)

P.V. Tobias (personal communication), commenting on a preliminary draft of this book, observed that the rather condensed presentation of 'natural selection' as contained in Julian Huxley's dictum, if not expanded upon could be misconstrued as being allied with the conventional assumption that Darwinian evolution is solely one of slow gradualism. Seen in this context it seemingly takes no account of theories of punctuated and reticulate evolution,[2] which have lately become prominent.

In practice, however, as P.V. Tobias himself has shown, these apparent innovations are but variations of the same Darwinian principle. Thus punctuated evolution merely implies a more explosive process of evolutionary change, which could be translated as an accelerated gradualism, with the explosive event occurring at a point where variations of species branch off the main stem to form new species. According to P.V. Tobias, one such point was reached in hominid evolution c. 2.5 million years ago when branching (or cladogenesis) occurred from the line of Australopithecus, producing the separate species of H. habilis, A. boisei, and A. robustus. (see Figure 6 – from P.V. Tobias 1982a)

P.V. Tobias further elucidates this point by referring to Simpson (1953), who has suggested that at the lowest level, the

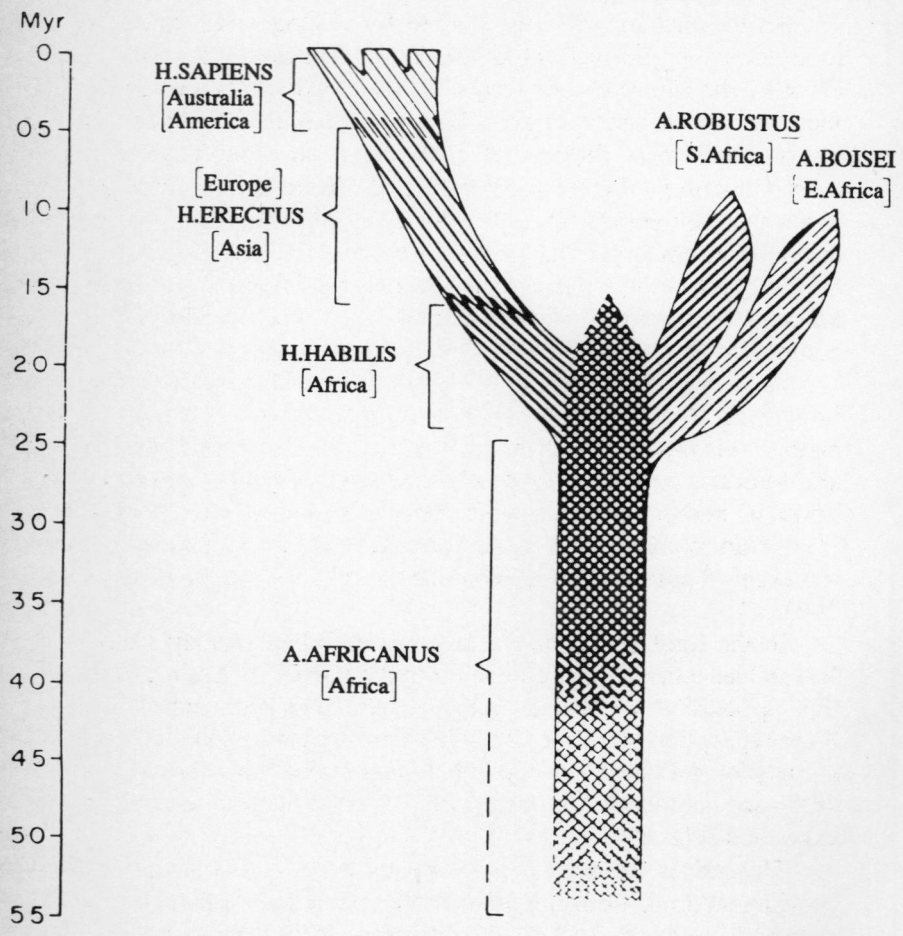

Figure 9. Provisional schema of hominid phylogeny showing the cladogenesis of just less than 2.5 millions of years ago: at that time there occurred a splitting of the hominid lineage from which flowed - in a moment of explosive evolution - three different species, H. habilis, A. robustus and A. bosei.

34

process of speciation 'starts usually with minor differences between individuals, which in most local populations fluctuate from generation to generation'.

As to what may be responsible for cladogenesis, or for a moment of explosive evolution, P.V. Tobias quotes Rench (1959), who in broad terms says of this question: 'The essential factor in the causation of such periods of explosive radiation is not an increase of the rate of mutation or an accumulation of macro-mutations, but an acceleration of differentiation, brought about by a temporary *intensification of selection* (my emphasis) due to environmental changes, e.g., by new types of vegetation or food resources, or due to colonization of new ranges with habitats unoccupied or inhabited by types inferior in competition.'

Referring to the 1859 and 1866 editions of Darwin's *Origin of Species*, P.V. Tobias also points out that Darwin's concept of evolution is inherent in both punctuational and gradual evolution and what has been called recently the theory of punctuated equilibria is not in variance with Darwin's theory or the neo-Darwinian synthesis, as some have held recently, but simply represents a special emphasis on one part of Darwinism' (Tobias 1983a).

In the light of the above, my use of Julian Huxley's term 'natural selection' and its meaning in the context of brain evolution is justified when adding the proviso that it covers all the three types of evolutionary change as elucidated by P.V. Tobias, namely – gradualist, punctational, and reticulate evolution – with an additional emphasis of the eliminative aspect as explained below.

This arises from further comments by P.V. Tobias on my provisional draft. Referring once more to J. Huxley's categorical statement on the role of natural selection, Tobias points out that it should not be forgotten that a great deal of evolutionary change could have been non-selective in character. He also notes that Julian Huxley himself stressed this point when speaking of the large role that non-selective accidental *elimination* (my emphasis), plays in evolution.

This argument strikes at a vital point of evolutionary theory to which I have repeatedly tried to draw attention, namely that the term 'natural selection' must be seen as a misnomer and that it describes in effect an act of 'natural elimination'.

Darwin came upon his theory of natural selection by first observing how animal and plant breeders selected chosen specimens for further breeding and thereby improved the race. This gave him the idea that a similar process might be going on in nature. So in order to distinguish deliberate man-made selection from the random natural process, he named it 'natural selection'.

But Darwin admitted later (see 1958 reprint), that correctly applied, the term natural selection was a misnomer, because human selection is a deliberate act, while, nature's process is not selective, but eliminative. Under conditions of nature – which additionally involve the Malthusian principle of proliferation in progeny, and the subsequent struggle for existence – the lesser adapted individuals will perish, while the better adapted will survive. In other words it is 'the survival of the fitter ones'.

In view of the above, I suggest that Huxley's original dictum to become all-embracing and generally applicable to biological evolutionary processes, should be enlarged as follows: *No evolutionary trend can be maintained except by natural selection – which in its true sense represents an act of natural elimination.*

And finally, Julian Huxley must have been aware of the basically eliminative aspect embodied in the term 'natural selection'. Otherwise he could not have made his original categorical and all-embracing statement.

It is this eliminative aspect we must keep in mind when we use the term natural selection.

How does this principle operate among animals in the wild, in humans, and finally in relation to human brain quality.[2] To take organic evolution as a whole, it can be observed (and this will later be shown in comparative death-rates) that practically all species of life, with the exception of modern humans and domesticated animals and plants, are subject to intensive natural selection (read natural elimination). In spite of this, however, most animal species have remained biologically constant.

Darwin (1958:66 reprint), observed that species will as a

36

rule not only remain constant over long periods of time but they will also frequently remain so under changed conditions of life. 'Certain Species,' he says, 'have migrated over vast spaces and have not become greatly or at all modified'.

There are living species and even genera of animals for which evolution seems virtually to have ceased for hundreds of million of years. One existing genus of 'Lingula', according to Rhodes (1962), has a history going back 500 million years. Other groups which have persisted over long periods of time are the lungfishes; the modern crocodiles, which differ little from crocodiles of the Jurassic period; and the opposums of South America, which closely resemble the small pouched mammals that had a world wide distribution 60 million years ago.

Soil insects such as spring-tails undergo practically no metamorphosis; they are wingless, and seem to be survivors from the epochs before insects had developed wings. An insect closely resembling them has been found in lower Devonian rocks in Scotland. It dates back some 300 million years, i.e., some 40–50 million years before the arrival of the earliest winged insects (Russel, 1966). Simson, quoted by Julian Huxley (1957), has said, 'an oyster from two hundred million years ago would look perfectly familiar to us if served in a restaurant today'.

The general principle that emerges is that an intensive natural selection pressure is necessary to keep animal species merely on an existing level of biological efficiency, or in other words, in a state of 'evolutionary constancy'. On the other hand, a decline in natural selection pressure is bound to lead to a reduction in biological quality.

Arriving at the hominids we can see the same principle at work. According to Gordon Childe (1966), for about 25,000 years man's bodily evolution has been virtually at a standstill. Men of the Aurignacian and Magdalenian cultures, compared with present-day men, show only negligible physiological differences, but their cultural difference is enormous. 'Progress in culture, in the human species,' he says, 'has replaced further organic evolution'.

Johanson (1982), speaking about A. afarensis says, 'They flourished from about 4 million years ago to about three million years ago. During that time they underwent little or no evolutionary change.' David Pilbeam (1960), discussing pre-Acheulian hominids, has pointed out that for a million years hominids seem to have not changed much except that brain size increased a little. W.W. Howells and E. Trinkaus (1980), refer to the remarkably long stability in the Neanderthalers physique. From the time of their full establishment, c. 100,000 years to c. 40–35,000 years ago, no evolutionary change can be noticed. Johanson (1982), describes Cro-Magnons found in southern France c. 40,000 years old to be virtually identical with humans of today.

While the above human examples refer mainly to periods of intensive natural selection, we must ask the question what happens to humans when natural selection pressure becomes less intense?

A comparative study of death-rates in animals and humans supplies a clue to this question. According to Kalmus (1964), only two out of 1000 of some insect species will on average reach maturity. This suffices to keep the species constant in numbers and biologically stable. To demonstrate the intensity of natural selection in nature, Darwin (1958), dug and cleared a piece of ground three feet long and two feet wide where there could be no choking influence from other plants. Then he marked all the seedlings of common weeds as they came up, and found that out of 375 no less than 295 were destroyed prematurely. Darwin also observed that the winter of 1854–5 destroyed four fifths (80%) of the birds on his grounds. He held this to be a case of tremendous destruction, considering that in human epidemics 10% is an extraordinarily severe mortality rate.

The intensity of natural selection in humans (or rather its lack) can be deduced from modern increases in life expectancy and thus comparative death rates, as well as from general population increases resulting from reduced death rates.

Average life expectancies from various historical times have been listed by A.J. Harrison (1967) as follows: (see also P.V. Tobias, 1982).

Early Bronze Age: 18 years
50 B.C.: 22 years
Middle Ages: 33 years
1687–91: 33 1/2 years

1789: 35 1/2 years
1838/1854: 40.9 years
1900/1902: 49.2 years
1946: 66.7 years

Figures showing increases in world-population have been advanced by C.H. Cippola (1965). They read:

Anno 1650 – 470 millions
1750 – 728 millions
1800 – 905 millions
1850 – 1.171 millions

1900 – 1.608 millions
1950 – 2.377 millions
1955 – 2.528 millions
2000 – 3.727 millions
(latest estimate c.6 billions)

In all societies, the largest proportion of deaths is usually due to infant mortality. In Europe, before this century, and in some less developed countries even now, of 1000 newborn children, 200 to 500 generally die before the age of seven (Cippola, 1965). However with preventive medicine, death rates amongst infants have been drastically reduced in most parts of the world. A. Barnett (1964), states that in England and Wales at the beginning of this century, sixty five out of every 100,000 children under fifteen died of diphtheria. Between the wars, with some children immunized, the figure fell to 29. In 1947, due to extensive immunization, the death rate was down to two per 100,000.

According to the *Daily Times*, Lagos, Nigeria (14.6.85), death rates in Nigeria dropped from 27 per thousand in the 1960s to 17 deaths per thousand in 1984. At the same time the infant mortality rate also declined from over 200 per thousand to 100 per thousand, while life expectancies increased from 35 to 55 years.[3]

Historically, world-wide, there has been a continuous decrease in death-rates in all age groups, running parallel with higher life expectancies and population increases, ever since Homo sapiens passed from the hunter and food-gathering stage of culture to one of agriculture and civilization. This process is tantamount to a progressive reduction in the intensity of natural selection. In other words, as cultural progress intensifies and expands, natural selection de-intensifies and decreases.

'The more elaborate social life is,' writes Julian Huxley (1957) 'the more it tends to shield individuals from the action of natural selection (i.e., the elimination of the lesser fit); and when this occurs, harmful mutations accumulate instead of being weeded out. As a result of this process, there can be no reasonable doubt that the human species today is burdened with many more deleterious mutant genes than can possibly exist in any species of wild creatures.' And I may add that such a process certainly disallows the qualitative improvement of any biological property be it physical or mental.

In modern civilization many biological deficiencies that natural selection would most likely have eliminated in former ages also survive through medical intervention. For example, many babies are born by Caesarian section and a too narrow uterus must therefore be considered as a congenital defect. In former times when sterile operational practice was still unknown, most pregnant women thus impeded would have died. However today the Caesarian procedure increases the survival of many infants, who when growing up, and in turn, producing children, are likely to pass this deficiency on to future generations. Acute appendicitis, or rather the inheritable tendency to it, presents a similar case.

According to Gerald Leach, one in every twenty-five babies is born with physical or mental handicap and lives. Survivors may procreate in later life and pass on these defects to their offspring.

He adds: 'These figures are bound to grow as scientists uncover the mostly mysterious causes of birth defects, some of which will be genetic. In fact it is widely estimated that for every known genetic effect, there are another three or four yet to be discovered.'

The many acute genetic defects (and others with only a hereditary pre-disposition) include diabetes, various eye ailments, dental caries and malocclusion, haemophilia, mongolism, and dwarfism, gout, pre-disposition to certain cancers, pancreatic disease, gastric and duodenal ulcers, rheumatic fever, deafness, etc. Also disturbing is an alarming increase in mental illness, noticeable in recent years throughout the civilized world.

Most of the above listed defects reflect major biological disorders. However when it comes to an examination of a possible decline in the intellectual level of an average population, we are dealing with much subtler influences, since the composite we call intelligence (or state of mind) depends on dozens of genetic determinants, each of them influencing the capacity of thinking or reasoning in a subtle and imperceptible way. A slight genetically induced imbalance will affect the brain quality of an individual and as such minor defects accumulate in the population there must be a general drop in the level of intelligence.

Is there any biological mechanism, apart from natural selection, which could prevent, or even counteract such a subtle mental decline? If there is, I am not aware of its existence. Nor has any workable alternative ever been proposed, apart from failed attempts of the Galton–Eugenists of the last century – not to forget Hitlerite attempts at racial purification.

But even if there was such a possibility and natural selection could be replaced by a rigorous eugenics orientated artificial selection or by means of genetic engineering, results would hardly be dramatic. We have shown that intensive selection in nature merely maintains the biological efficiency of a species, and artificial man-made selection, if at all practicable, could not do much more.

The reader may object that the above does not present the entire picture, and that while constancy of species is an established fact in organic life, the less frequent emergence of new variations and species is an indication that viable biological changes in organisms are possible. Indeed, we can even monitor the processes which can lead to biological change. For example, J.M. Smith (1966), has shown that the simplest genetic change in a population is the replacement at a locus of one allele by another insofar as natural selection leads to the extinction of individuals carrying the less favourable allele.

J.B.S. Haldane has calculated that a great number of selective deaths, spread over many generations, are required, before one allele has replaced another. He found that unless selection was very intense, the number of selective deaths equalled about ten to 100 times. Haldane maintained that an intensity of selection of 0.01 is a more probable figure, and if so it would take 3,000 generations of selection to replace one allele by another. Further species probably differ by alleles at about 1000 loci (that is, the number is probably greater than 100 and less than 10,000). If so, the evolution of a new species would take about 300,000 generations. While this figure may perhaps be exaggerated, it emphasises the great intensity of natural selection that is required to affect evolutionary changes.

We can therefore imagine the many generations needed to deliberately increase mental qualities in human beings by genetic manipulation – if such were at all possible.

What the above examples most specifically indicate is that when left to chance (i.e., in absence of any deliberate selection), as it has been left throughout the history of all culturally advanced societies, both before and since, *no automatic increase in the brain's intellectual qualities can be expected*. On the contrary, as we have shown, a decrease in natural selection standards, must lead to an increase of adverse mutations in a population, and thus towards a lower level of mental efficiency – or at the most optimistic assumption to a standstill in its mental level.

The causes involved become apparent when we compare Stone Age humans with their modern counterparts. Under the former's conditions, all energies seem to have been concentrated on survival in an assumedly harsh environment with the aid of primitive cultural means, necessitating an alertness and intelligence certainly sharper than that required under civilization where a sophisticated arsenal of tools, weapons, implements, and the protective embrace of modern society, with an elaborate medical science to back it, make living less severe. In addition, the store of increasing knowledge, passed on from generation to generation and incessantly added to, becomes available to most members of our civilized world, irrespective of their genetic make-up, and often replaces the need for greater intelligence.[4] Today, the weak, the foolish, the non-alert, and the naive, can and do survive.

In such an environment there is no selective process which prevents the mentally less endowed individuals from procreating. Consequently the intellectual level in modern populations is much more likely to decrease, than to increase.

As Brace/Montague (1968) have correctly pointed out: 'In literate societies, with an elaborate division of labour, the average level of intelligence in terms of pure survival value is probably lower than in cultures where the problems of survival are much more immediate. The premium placed on human intelligence in face of prolonged scarcity in the Australian desert, or at the edge of the polar ice-cap where the penalty for stupidity is death, is almost certainly greater than it is even for the most down-trodden inhabitant of Western Europe or Northern America.'

The same authors point out however that there are mitigating factors which prevent the mental level of a population from dropping below a certain level. With the social limitations which total mental incompetence imposes on its bearers, men and women below a certain level (i.e., idiots) are unlikely to have the chance to produce children.

It should now be clear to the reader that the cultural gains of early, as well as modern civilization (including perhaps the Mezolithic – and Neolithic sequences as well), have been achieved in spite of stagnating, and possibly, even of declining brain qualities!

It is significant to note that P.V. Tobias has come to similar, though not identical conclusions. In a general assessment of human evolution and culture (*The Antiquity of Man*, 1982), he writes:

'It is suggested that the main natural selective advantage flowing from brain enlargement and specially of the lower frontal, lower parietal, and upper temporal regions, was the evolution of mechanisms for the transmission of culture, and that means primarily cognitive abilities and articulate speech. By making possible a new kind of inheritance, cultural or social inheritance, articulate speech facilitated the learning of the new techniques by children of the next generation. It took the universal mammalian capacity for learned behaviour and refined it into a powerful mechanism for insuring survival. The survival of future generations is exactly what evolution is all about.

'The feedback system operated for approximately 150,000 generations (c. 2.2 million years – G.K.) ... when these advanced stages were reached, the whole process slowed down. Beyond a certain point of cultural evolution (which should rather be read as 'cultural development', G.K.), it was no longer an advantage to have bigger and better brains. Cultural sharing and the benevolence of social life had taken the place of nimble wits of the individuals as an insurance against extinction. Encephalization (i.e., the enlargement of the brain – G.K.) was no longer at a premium. One could manage and be as educable with 1,250 g. of brain as with 2,250g.'

ANSWERS TO SOME OBJECTIONS RAISED

It may be observed that our brain curve (see pages pp.75-77) is based on the rather simplistic expedient of pure brain size, without taking account of body size – i.e., cc/h (cc for cm3, and h for height). But as the values obtained by the latter method are only marginally different, they do not affect the conclusions drawn. As a matter of fact, using the coefficient[5] for phylogenetical brain-capacity, it even emphasizes the relatively greater brain capacities of earlier hominids. As hominids evolved it can be observed that body size (expressed in average height) increased, so that relative brain capacities of later hominids actually decreased. This is particularly noticeable in post-Neanderthal/Upper-Palaeolithic prototypes.

For example, a computation of relative brain capacities set out in Table 2 of a treatise by O.J. Grusser and L.R. Weiss (1985) gives the following values: Homo sapiens neanderthalensis mean brain size, 1487 cc; average body height 165 cm; and a resulting capacity computation of 9.012. The same indicators given for H. sapiens sapiens, read: –1345–172–7.82. Yet in the progress of this argument the authors are trying to predict an almost automatic rise in brain capacities in future generations. This is based on the assumption that further phylogenetic growth of the brain will result from an increase of the cortical brain cells.

44

This seems to have been based on the further assumption that the intellectual demands of modern life in an expanding scientific and technological civilization, are apt to increase the size of the brain, and perhaps the intellectual capacities as well. It is not denied, that the greater use of the brain can increase its capacities, just as the greater use of a muscle will increase its strength. What the authors seem to have neglected is the fact that this simply means the greater use of an already existing, inborn, (though limited) range, of brain powers – hitherto greatly under used. What the authors further seem to have overlooked is that the inherited range is genetically determined and limited; and that it cannot be changed by mental exercise. To assume therefore that a phylogenetic increase in brain capacities could be obtained by a greater use of the brain (or of any other organ), and that this could in retrospect become inheritable, means a return to Lamarckian inheritance. In reality, increase in inheritable brain capacities would only be possible by means of natural, or artificial selection, a factor which has been discussed in the preceding text, or by genetic manipulation.

Admittedly the necessarily condensed treatment of natural selection as submitted here is vulnerable to criticisms in detail. One, a personal communication has already been dealt with in footnote 4 (p.145). Another prominent critic raises the interesting question of genetic influences on selection. He suggests ... 'you will need to examine how your arguments are affected by modern genetic theory which embraces neutral mutations and which does not regard selection as operating at the species level, in the sense that "effects" of any selection are on individuals. Modern theory also suggests that genetic change is, to a large extent, "built into" the genetic code; natural selection is thought to operate to impose some direction on a series of otherwise random effects.'

The above observations may be debated on several grounds. Firstly, neutral mutations emerging in the hereditary make-up of individuals or species are obviously more frequent if the selection pressure declines, which is the case in modern humans. Should the selection pressure intensify, a factor which rather applies more to pre-modern humans, some of the formerly

45

neutral mutations would either have proved useful and been preserved, or if proved deleterious, they, and the individuals bearing them, would eventually have been eliminated.

Secondly, the assumption that there is a directive element in the genetic make-up of humans or any other species, is unlikely, because natural selection, being de-facto an eliminative process, automatically excludes any directive motivation. Furthermore, if such a genetically inspired directive influence were operative in the brain of the modern humans it would also have had to be already present throughout the entire range of pre-human animal ancestors, since certainly all these animal species would have greatly benefitted by greater brain powers. Yet thousands of animal species have stagnated in their brain evolution over enormous periods of time despite being subject to much greater natural selection pressure than are civilized humans.

Even the culturally most primitive hunter-gatherers extant are now recognized as fully fledged H. sapiens. Therefore, why should they have stagnated on a culturally under-developed level for tens of thousands of years, when a directive brain element in their make-up should have driven them to perform cultural feats, equalling those of their civilized counterparts? Also there apparently exists no genetical evidence to hint at the presence of a directive element in the brain's anatomy, either by natural selection or otherwise.

Genetically based objections to my argument on natural-selection, about the increased intellectual qualities, supposedly to be automatically operative in modern humans, are also unlikely to be valid. All genetic effects, as well as any still to be discovered, have been operative ever since organic life appeared on earth. Darwin knew nothing of genetics, yet he demonstrated in his Origin of Species that natural selection in all its different manifestations was the principal agent in transmuting organic life, whether affecting individuals, species, or genera, and in my view irrespective of their genetic make-up.

Although many attempts have been made to discredit Neo-Darwinian Theory (which rests on the action of natural selection plus genetic inheritance) – by a revival of what may be called Neo-Lamarckism, they are all quite unconvincing.[6] Moreover, in this respect, the postulation of a directive element in brain evolution unmistakably has a Lamarckian taint.

Modern genetics and more so genetical engineering have increasingly shown that there is no mechanism in the gene equipment to accommodate any Lamarckian type of inheritance. Yet Neo-Lamarckists, having lately become quite vocal in the biological field, have tried every subterfuge to infiltrate some Lamarckian principles into the biological evolutionary pantheon. I do not deny that there are certain aspects of organic evolution which so far have defied explanations based on natural selection (better called natural elimination) alone. If there is another as yet unknown influence involved beside natural selection (i.e. elimination) to explain the origin of species it is most unlikely that it can be based on Lamarckian inheritance. Furthermore, even if there should be any additional influences working at certain stages of the evolutionary process (like the perfection of the eye), they would still have to be subject to the discriminating agency of natural selection (or elimination) as the final arbiter.

I conclude by citing Dean Falk (1980). Commenting on the dramatic increase in brain size during hominid evolution, he concludes (1980): 'Because of human technology, language and the mental faculties for conscious deliberate abstract thought that these achievements imply, H. sapiens appears to be qualitatively more intelligent than even his "closest" non-human primate relatives. Yet the search for qualitative brain differences that separate fossils and living hominids from pongids has been futile. It may be that qualitative differences exist at micro (e.g., neurochemical) levels and are not reflected in the gross paleo-neurological evidence. If so, the field of comparative neurology (e.g., Armstrong 1979, 1980) is more likely than paleoneurology to contribute to our knowledge of qualitative human brain evolution.' In the meantime, Falk suggests, that at least for the hominid brain, bigger was better.

Further, I may add that Homo sapiens, the hominid with the biggest brain, reached an average brain size of 1350 cc. probably between 300,000 and 200,000 years ago. This is the same average size at which modern contemporary humans (on a world scale) are assessed. Altogether this suggests a stasis in brain development which more or less continued over the entire c. 300,000 years of Homo sapiens existence. So far no anatomical or genetically based evidence has been produced to show that the functional, or intellectual potential of modern humans has increased, during the last 10,000 years. And while it is not denied that future research may yet produce such evidence, I estimate the chances for this to happen as very slim.

7. THE SYNDROME OF CULTURAL UNDER-DEVELOPMENT

What do we mean by cultural under-development? It is well known that apes are incipient tool-users and that we can perhaps speak of a rudimentary ape-culture, even involving the teaching of their young. Furthermore, the ape's cultural aptitudes cannot be considered a novel acquirement and probably have persisted unchanged over many millions of years. Some hominids have expanded on this by developing stone tool technologies. These became increasingly more elaborate, passing through the stages of simple pebble tools (Hadar and Oldowan) followed by the Acheulian, Mousterian, Upper Palaeolithic and Neolithic sequences, with all their known variations and refinements. It appears however, that only a limited portion of hominids partook in these lithic developments, Homo sapiens included.

The question is, why should members of the biologically uniform species Homo sapiens have taken two different cultural trajectories; one portion remaining culturally under-developed for hundreds of thousands of years and the other progressing culturally through various stages, climaxing in modern civilization.

In broad terms 'Cultural Under-Development' as applied

here, refers to the bulk of those hunter-gatherers groups, contemporary as well as prehistoric, who still live, or once lived, below the cultural level of agricultural and stock-rearing societies.

THE HUNTER-GATHERERS

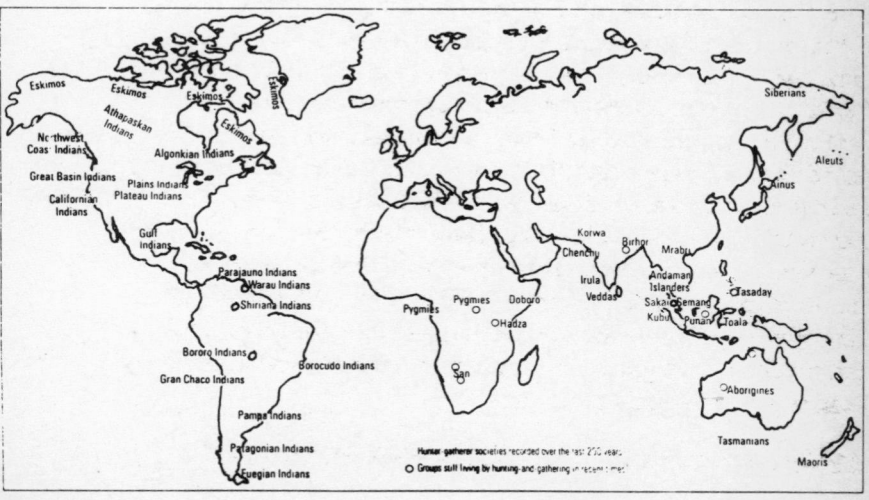

Figure 10. Most of the world's people adopted agriculture 10,000 years ago. Some exceptions were the North American natives and the Aboriginals of Australia who remained hunter-gatherers. Of those who were still hunting and gathering 200 years ago very few remain today, and many who have persisted with this form of life are being forced by government agencies into settlement. Our ancestors were hunter-gatherers up to four million years ago, and those who still are find their way of life threatened by `civilization'.
From R. Leakey: *The Making of Mankind*.

Writing about the economy of prehistoric hunter-gatherers Geof Bailey (1983: Foreword), points out that human societies have spent over 99% of their cultural history as hunters and gatherers. Others, including Bitchery (1972) and Gowlett (1984), have expressed similar views. Of interest also is Richard Leakey's opinion (1981) that early hominids were perhaps more gatherers than hunters, and therefore he proposed to call them 'gatherer-hunters', while George Carter suggests the name 'forager'.

What is significant is that these culturally less complex hominids roamed the globe for the best part of four million years, up to c. 10,000 years ago, when village life and farming began to make inroads on their hunter-gatherer existence. Remarkable is the fact that some hunter-gatherer populations survived into our age, retaining a life style which, in some respects, may resemble that of their prehistoric forebears. During this large time span cultural progress was minimal.

Until about fifty years ago such survivors were said to have included the Mbuti of the Congo; Kung-San of South Africa; Veddahs of Ceylon; various jungle tribes of S. India; Semang of Malaya (Negritos); Sakai, Senoi, and Jakun of Malaya (Australoid); Andaman Islanders; Kunu of Sumatra; Punan of Borneo; various Eskimo tribes of the northern hemisphere; Paiute of Nevada, Utah and Arizona; Indigenes of California; inhabitants of the Tierra del Fuego and assorted Australian aborigines; etc. These examples are of the most diverse racial stock and represent every possible climatic region.

It would however be a mistake to lump all those described as hunter-gatherers into one cultural entity. Although they cannot be strictly separated from one another culturally, it is convenient to divide them into three categories.[1]

Into the 'First Category' I propose to include those who have been least affected by their sedentary or pastoral neighbours, either by a refusal to become assimilated, or due to less accessible habitats. Among those probably least affected by outside influences are the two Mbuti dwarf people, or pygmies, of the Congo and the lesser known dark-skinned forest-dwarfs of Malaya, the Kubu of Sumatra, the Punan of Borneo, and the Semang of Malaya, to mention just a few. As to their material culture, their mere survival into the modern age compels us to conclude that their way of life is highly adapted to their environment and in no way inferior in survival value to that of their culturally more complex contemporaries.

R. Lee, (cited by R. Leakey, 1981), known for his extensive

studies of hunter-gatherer societies, offered that as a general rule foraging people on the whole deploy tremendous skill and only minimal technology in exploiting their environment. 'They live in such a harmonious relationship with nature that the hunter-gatherer way of life can be described as the most successful adaptation man has ever achieved.' Edmund Leach, goes further. He wrote (in correspondence) that 'nobody in their senses would live in any other way if they had the space'.

The 'Second Category' includes hunter-gatherers already more deeply affected by foreign influences. Prominent among these are the Kung-San (Bushmen) of Southern Africa. However, they still reveal ostensibly authentic facets of a socio-logically and ideologically unpolluted life-style reminiscent of the above 'Category One'.

'Category Three' comprises that multitude of hunter-gatherers who have already accepted a great part of the way of life of their sedentary agricultural neighbours. (They are listed in footnote 1, p.146) Desmond Clark comments (*Man the Hunter*, 1968): 'Most of the hunter-gatherer groups existing today are living in some of the least favourable habitats and have long been in contact with more complex societies and technologies. They can therefore no longer be considered 'typical' or useful for any comparison with prehistoric populations'. I suggest that some of those listed in categories one and two above, are exceptions to this generalization.

By occasionally describing the 'First Category' of hunter-gatherers as cultural primitives or even ultra-primitives, I try to contrast them with the more acculturated ones belonging to category two and three. It needs stressing that the above descriptions do not imply an inferior type of culture or intellect but one that is less complex or sophisticated.

ASPECTS OF EVOLUTIONARY TRANSITION

It is generally held that Homo sapiens emerged c. 300,000 years ago as the evolutionary successor of Homo erectus. And although the circumstances of this biological transformation have so far remained obscure, we can assume that certain gene mutations in erectus were more amenable to natural selection thus leading to the new species Homo sapiens. On the other hand the genetically less adapted erectus became extinct.

In speculating how natural selection could have effected this evolutionary change both biological and cultural factors must be considered. Here the earlier evolution of the hominids offers some clues. It has been proposed that the emergence of hominids from the primates was perpetuated by two principal factors, bi-pedalism and enlarged cranial capacities. Bi-pedalism freed the hands for tool-use. In addition, certain changes in the hand's anatomy provided greater agility and further, the development of articulate speech helped to promote intercommunication and the passing on of experience to future generations.

The evolutionary transition from erectus to sapiens was not paralleled by any noticeable change in stone-tool technology — and we have no other really suitable cultural parameter. The use of fire, a major cultural achievement, occurred much too sporadically to be considered as a comparative measure, with its earliest use traced to Chesowanja in the Rift-Valley, c. 1½ million years ago (Gowlett, 1984).[2] Another prominent cultural achievement, the bow and arrow, is also unsuitable for comparative purposes, with its earliest use presumed to date back to only 40,000 years, as deduced from finds of early microlites in S. Africa (Gowlett, 1984), indicating their use as arrow-points.

The Acheulian hand-axe tradition which for a million years had been closely connected with Homo erectus (both culture and hominid dating from about the same time c. 1½ million years ago) continued unabated far into Homo sapiens' era. Therefore if we fix the advent of Homo sapiens around the acceptable figure of c. 300,000 years ago, we find that it took another almost 150,000 years before the Acheulian hand-axe technology (having become more refined and sophisticated as time went by), gave way to the new and more varied Mousterian stone tool technology. The latter became the prerogative of Homo sapiens neanderthalensis. Both, technology and hominid, emerged c. 150,000 years ago.

Lacking therefore any cultural signpost which could give us

52

a clue as to how homo sapiens entered the evolutionary scene, we must resort to anatomy (see diagram DI p.78). Here the likely factor is an increase in average cranial capacities from c. 1000 cc. of erectus to the c. 1350 cc. of sapiens. When exactly this biological transformation occurred is obscure. It was likely gradual, stretching over many millennia, with the process possibly completed between c. 0.75 and 0.25 million years B.P. (Tobias, 1986). John Gowlett writes (1984): '700,000 years ago we find only H. erectus, but by 200,000 years ago we find mainly Homo sapiens'.

Here we note the most intriguing aspect of contemporary hunter-gatherers. Their status as fully fledged Homo sapiens (and sapiens sapiens) is now accepted by all modern biologists. This includes all the above mentioned categories, and they are confirmed as our biological equals, both physically and intellectually.

STONE-TOOL DEVELOPMENTS

As indicated previously, there is a consensus amongst anthropologists that the manufacture of durable tools (i.e. the lithic cultural phases) and their improvement and perfection (refinement), can be used as a measuring rod for cultural progress throughout the Stone-Age, being part and parcel of a *cultural evolutionary* process. It is assumed that the first step in this direction was taken c. 2½ million years ago or even earlier.

Evidence for this progression is seen in a stone-tool technology of increasing elaboration and refinement, supplying almost the only cultural permanency preserved in the archaeological record of the c. 2½ million years of the Stone Age. During this time, stone tool technology, progressed from the pebble tools of H. afarensis and H. habilis to the Acheulian hand-axe complex, followed by the more elaborate Mousterian tools, continuing with the further refinements of the Upper Palaeolithics and ending with the polished stone implements of the Neolithic – all these stages showing great variety, while seemingly projecting a continuous evolutionary trajectory.

Closer scrutiny, however, reveals that the process was far

from smooth, nor is it applicable to all mankind. This is evidenced in (a.) long period of uneven progress, even stasis and recession; and (b.) the absence of any stone-tool making altogether, even among some modern hunter-gatherer survivors.

Case (a.): The Oldowan pebble tool complex of H. habilis persisted seemingly unchanged for c. a million years, to be superseded by the Acheulian (Ach.) hand-axe complex. Several authors among them Richard Leakey (1981), have observed that the Acheulian tool-kit emerged first c. $1^{1/2}$ million years ago, and that the basic design persisted until c. 200,000 B.P. In Africa it was followed by the more complex Middle Stone-Age Acheulian technology, while in W. Europe it is in evidence as late as 100,000 B.P. During the entire $1^{1/2}$ million years of the Acheulian there was no marked refinement to be seen, and some of the later examples of Acheulian stone-tools appear even simpler and cruder compared to earlier ones. Though there were differences from region to region, variation was not dramatic. Leakey concludes that we have here the startling fact of H. erectus technology being little changed during the entire $1^{1/2}$ million years.

Johanson (1982), similarly observed that after the Acheulian industry appeared suddenly c. $1^{1/2}$ million years ago it evolved little thereafter, stubbornly resisting change for a million years. Clark and Piggott (1970) comment that: 'Even the most perfect finished hand-axe presented no more than the culmination of the process of refining a primitive chopper-tool'. Liam de Paor (1971), among others wrote, 'All that can be traced in stone tool development is the painfully slow improvement in technique of a few simple tools, over millions of years'. And finally, R. Leakey (1981): 'If one considers the stone implements made by our ancestors over the past couple of million years, an interesting paradox emerges: although there is a steady increase in the number of identifiable tool-types, together with a refinement of the individual implements, the *range* of artefacts does not broaden significantly until about 40,000 years ago when new and more delicate types of tools appear. In other words, even in the very earliest toolkits one can find edges, points, surfaces and so on that are features of the basic implements of stone tool cultures right up to the late Stone-Age'.

Case (b.) This involves both the absence as well as the abandonment of stone tool making among modern hunter-gatherers, as well as the use of stone tools inferior to those H. habilis used and made c. 2 million years earlier. The following are illustrative examples. Firstly, there are the Mbuti dwarf-people (pygmies) of the Ituri Forest in the Congo, as described by Colin Turnbull (1983). In a review of their economy he describes it as incorporating a pre-stone tool technology.

He elucidates that to the best of his knowledge, the Mbuti (possibly in living memory), used no stone tools whatsoever.[4] They find it cumbersome to deal with them when lighter materials are at hand which can be fashioned with less effort to do the same job. Turnbull also observed that the Mbuti occasionally find stone tools lodged in old trees or buried in the ground (perhaps dating from the earlier Sagoen culture). They show little interest, and certainly have no need whatsoever to use them, let alone to make them.

About the stone-tool, propensities of the Ik a mountain people in northern Uganda, Turnbull informs me that unlike the Mbuti, they live in an environment with abundant stone, where stone tools ready-made by nature abound, i.e., splinters broken from rocks, smoothed by being tumbled down ravines during flash-floods, sharpened by being chipped against each other, etc. 'I never saw them making stone-tools.'

They purposely chose what may be called 'pebble-tools, because, they said, they are more comfortable to hold in the palm of the hand, as they could strike with them much harder than they could perhaps with sharper stones that did not have a smooth face to fit comfortable into the palm. They used stone-tools for hammers, for cutting, for slicing, but rarely for chopping – for which they preferred to use metal'. Before, or in the absence of metal they would obviously have used suitable stone debris as explained further on below.

Another example of the casual use of stones for tools is cited by Daryl Forde (1968), in the context of the culturally lowly Semang of Malaya. 'The splitting and scraping of wood is generally done with rough shapeless stones, picked up at need and thrown away again. Indeed, it is doubtful whether an archaeologist finding the remains of a Semang hearth, after the wooden tools have rotted away in the hot, humid climate, would in the few rough stones recognize a human industry at all'.

In evaluating stone tools therefore, one needs to distinguish between the use of unworked, casually picked up stones and stones deliberately shaped by human hand. According to Gowlett (1984), flaking is not normally used to produce a sharp edge but rather one which is strong and regular – for nothing is sharper than an unworked fresh edge of a splinter, which can cut an elephant-skin as effectively as a steel knife. But such handling is of course much clumsier and prone to injure the unprotected hand. Nevertheless, in the absence of metal, stone splinters of various shapes and sizes are suited to cut meat and sinews and shape wood and bone. Nick Toth, a practitioner in stone tools, tells us that with sharp stone flakes one can do almost any aspect of butchering. Simple lava flakes can even penetrate the hide of an elephant, which is almost 2.5 cm (1") thick. However, says Toth, one needs a large number of flakes to do so and this demands great patience while the hands will also get sore. (Quoted by R. Leakey, 1981.)

THE CULTURE COMPLEX OF HOMO HABILIS

Doubtless, the cultural achievements of even the earliest hominids may go far beyond the abilities we can assess from their crude stone-tool remains alone. Yet archaeological remains other than stone, pointing to such hidden capacities, are rare due to the perishable nature of the material they may have used.

However, partly by inference I propose that P.V. Tobias' (1983a) summary of the cultural aptitutes of Homo habilis cited below is one of the most impressive statements so far made about the cultural beginnings of this first 'Homo' species, between c. 2.3 and c. 1.7 million years ago.

P.V. Tobias writes that the cultural assemblages of Homo habilis have been designated as Oldowan (M.D. Leakey 1971). Among the stone tools there was a predominance of choppers of which five types, side, end, two-edged, pointed and chisel-edged have been described. Other forms included proto-bifaces, polyhedrons, discoids, spheroids, heavy-duty and light-duty scrapers, burins and sundry other tools. 'To this variegated suite of tool-types must be added the evidence that Homo habilis was capable of constructing some form of shelter in the form at least of stone-walling. The implemental and constructional activities bespeak a complex culture'. Evidence suggests that 'the culture of Homo habilis included the aimed throwing of missiles,[5] the butchery of large animal carcasses with stone tools, the transport of meat and other foods to a home base, delayed consumption, the sharing of food and the distribution of the meat to adult and juvenile members of the group (M.D. Leakey, 1971; Issaac, 1978). All in all, the cultural achievements, both those observed and those inferred, imply a high degree of intelligent activity and could hardly have taken place without the assistance of some form of speech'.

It is noteworthy that we find most of the activities outlined above (with the exception of Homo habilis' elaborate stone-tool technology), incorporated in the life-style of many modern hunter-gatherers, with the addition, of course, of intrusive cultural elements derived over the millennia from culturally more complex populations. Consequently, considering modern hunter-gatherer populations of a primitive cultural level (our categories one and two), I conclude that during the more than two million years which have elapsed since Homo habilis' beginnings, their cultural progress has been minimal, and in terms of implied cultural evolution it was practically nil. And yet modern hunter-gatherers are fully fledged Homo sapiens, sharing with us an average brain capacity of c. 1350 cc., which is more than double that computed for Homo habilis, of 646 cc., (P.V. Tobias 1983a).

The comparative picture becomes particularly pertinent if we use the standard of stone-tool technology as a cultural and intellectual parameter. In this respect, the Mbuti (without any stone-tool making propensities) would have to be considered as ranging culturally and intellectually below Homo habilis of more than 2 million years ago. Yet, as the observations of Colin Turnbull show, the Mbuti cannot be considered intellectually inferior to contemporary civilized populations, though they lag

Chopper

Heavy duty scraper

Chopper

Burin

Light duty scraper

Beaked point

Discoid

Polyhedron

Figure 11. Tools from the Oldowan industry, excavated from Olduvai Gorge. The Oldowan industry is the earliest identifiable collection of tools, first made around two million years ago.

behind in cultural complexity and sophistication. Observes R.L. Holloway (1984): 'Were modern living human hunters and gatherers to be judged on the basis of stone-tool technology alone, they would probably be considered less advanced "brain-wise", than Neanderthalers'.

Among the Mbuti, Turnbull informs me, their economy requires a minimum technology, still at a stone age level. In the use of indigenous tools (other than stone), they are highly adaptive and adaptable, but the degree of their adaptation is light by the very nature of their life and environment which has remained stable for many thousands of years – and may, under similar environmental conditions have resembled in many though not in all respects that of prehistoric hunter-gatherer populations during most of the stone age. The most conspicuous prehistoric achievements of the latter, being the making and use of fire and the bow and arrow; besides possessing, most importantly, the full capacity for articulate speech as evolved in Homo habilis and perfected in Homo sapiens.

In adjudging the Mbuti's intellectual level, Turnbull remarks, 'My observations in this field were that in intelligence many Mbuti seemed to have a far higher I.Q. than I, and some were exceptionally dumb in some respects and exceptionally bright in others. The kind of variation I may expect in any population I happen to know. All of them seemed to have far greater knowledge and understanding of the world they lived in than most of us in our complex western world'.

Such cultural assessments of modern, culturally 'underdeveloped' hunter-gatherers, raises another important question. If such groups, as we know, managed to survive comfortably into our age (particularly so while remaining reasonably sheltered from culturally more complex intrusions), and using perhaps only a few pebble tools, or none at all; *is it not possible that this low cultured-type of Homo (including the biological species, of Homo habilis, Homo erectus, and even early Homo sapiens) formed the majority of hunter-gatherers in prehistoric times, while stone-tool makers, particularly those with an elaborate technology, formed a minority?*

Attempting to reach a positive conclusion I offer this as a theory worthy of consideration.

This theory is based on the presumed presence of hominids in areas with ample food resources, yet devoid of specific stone-tool finds or human fossil remains. These hypothetical populations comprise those multitudes of ancient hunter-gatherers of different hominid species who must have populated the intermediate areas between known stone tool and hominid fossil locations. The Homo habilis sites in East and South Africa are good examples, and some are pinpointed on a D. Johanson map of the Old World (1982). Among them the Olduvai site just south of the northern Tanzanian border, is separated from the next marked Homo habilis site to the south, in the Transvaal, by c. 3000 km. Both groups, being of the species Homo habilis must in consequence have almost certainly been in physical contact at some point in time and must therefore have traversed, or possibly occupied, parts of this huge intermediate expanse during many millennia, though leaving no trace thus far, in the form of stone-tools, of their presence.

The distribution of Homo erectus, throughout the same or other areas, with his much more abundant Acheulian hand-axe assemblies, is, subject to the same principle. R. Leakey has suggested that the Acheulian stone industry at Olduvai was the fountainhead from which other Acheulian sites, derived their cultural capital. In his opinion (1981),: 'The Acheulian industry continued, with steady refinements right to the end of the sequence at Olduvai. And when some African hominids migrated north, they took their technology with them'. Subsequently, we witness the widespread Acheulian presence, in North Africa, Egypt, Europe and Asia. Their dispersal seems to coincide with the spread of Homo erectus from 1½ million years onwards.

H. erectus fossils have been located in Tanzania, South Africa, Morocco, Algeria, Germany, Hungary, China and Java. As in the previous example of Homo habilis there exist large intermittent areas between the known tool assemblies of Homo erectus, which the species must have occupied during their dispersal. These areas being void of any sign of Homo erectus activity (i.e., void of stone-tool finds), must be considered subject to the same previously mentioned principle which assumes that said areas must have been populated by countless generations of non stone-tool making Homo erectus hunter-gatherers, but with no remains accounting for their presence during this particular time sequence.

A striking example in support of my theory is *Homo erectus javanensis*, or Pithecanthropus. This hominid left only fossils but no tools (G.v. Bonin, 1963), while his evolutionary relative in distant China (Sinanthropus) left fossils as well as an ample supply of stone tools: cores, flakes and scrapers – though there were no Acheulian type hand-axes present. (Clark/Piggott, 1970).

Discussing the distribution of hand-axes in Europe, McBurney (1967) speaks of their densest occurrence in certain areas of Spain, France and Britain. In contrast, he points out the lowland zone between Elbe and Rhine, c. 200 miles (320 km) long, with only sporadic traces of hand-axe assemblies. Furthermore the whole of Central Europe and the Euroasiatic plain appears uninhabited although the area has supported, locally, many of the animals hunted by hand-axe makers elsewhere.

The Neanderthalers who follow Homo erectus in the evolutionary scale show the same tendency of isolated tool-making activities. Discussing at length the spread of the West and East European Mousterian flake-tool assemblies in Europe McBurney (1967), recognizes them as successors of the Acheulian hand-axe industry: 'The Eastern Mousterian can be detected over a wide area of East and Central Europe, from the Rhine to the Oxus basin in the western bastions of the Himalaya'. A detailed study of tool distribution reveals wide gaps between known tool assemblies in areas with ample food-resources, while the same to a lesser degree applies to the Upper-Palaeolithic populations who followed the Neanderthalers. 'Their beginning are evidenced mainly on the European Continent from c. 50,000 B.P. onwards'. Their varying cultural expressions and spread have been detailed in Chapter 5.

In attempting to assess the stone-tool histories of prehistoric hominids over the last two million years, I am submitting a set of the following, somewhat speculative, figures which may at least hint at the true state of affairs.

Assuming that each generation counted 5 million people throughout the entire period (J. Campbell, 1983, proposed 10 million for a world population, predating the Neolithic), with each generation lasting 15 years, (P.V. Tobias, 1982) we obtain a total pre-agricultural population of c. 750,000 millions (750 billions).

Now estimating that every one in ten of these stone-age beings produced an average of 500 tools during his lifetime (admittedly debatable figures but they serve a purpose here), the total number of stone-tools would have numbered 37,500 billions. Estimating further that the combined weight of 5000 stone-tools (large and small combined) approximates one ton (1000 kg.), the total stone-tool tonnage would have amounted to 2,500 billion tons!

Even if this figure appears highly inflated and the real amount were only a fraction of it our landscape (particularly where raw materials for stone-tools are located) would have to be dotted with large hills of stone-tools, at least in the millions, if not in billions, of tons.

Still, although we can hardly speak of millions of tons, there are places where large masses of stone debris, mixed with finished stone-tools, indicate an abundance of past stone-tool making activities. George Carter (personal communication) tells me that he has seen quarries in U.S.A. that cover acres with flake debris many feet deep. One quarry is one mile long and the debris are piled up the sides. Further, one area in Georgia, has so much flake debris that it shows up as a large whitish area from the air, while the flake debris and artifacts around ancient lake Lahotan run for miles along the lake shore. In the Mohave desert near the Calico site flake debris are scattered over at least 100 square miles. Carter also records that some areas in Australia show an abundance of stone debris as a residue from stone-workings.

An African example is the Kilombe area in Kenya where up to 100 tons of stone tools, mainly hand-axes, covering a wide area, have been found (Gowlett, 1984). Another African location in Kenya recorded by R. Leakey (1981), is the site of Olorgesailis in the Rift Valley, where Glynn and Barbara Isaak found more than 10,000 well made hand-axes, littered among the remains of giant baboons. Also, according to R. Leakey, from a cave at Dragon Bone Hill at Choucoutien in China (a site near Peking), 20,000 stone-tools were excavated, together with forty H. erectus specimen, the dating being c. 500,000 B.P.

Even so, measured relative to hominid global spread throughout the millions of years of the palaeolithic (stone-age), the conclusions emerging from the above account suggest that stone-tool making may have been the preserve of only a minority of hominids, although in the areas where stone-tools were actually made their presence seems quite prolific. The majority of hominids although not inferior in their physique or intelligence, seem to have got along quite comfortably without making any stone-tools, just as did the Kwa-Mbuti of the Congo until recent history. It is also quite obvious, as sporadic evidence indicates, that practically all hominids used stones as tools throughout the entire stone age, though in a casual manner, not bothering to knap them into shape. This is further corroborated by the examples of some, until recently surviving hunter-gatherers (detailed above) who, although using stone debris for tools, showed no inclination to trim them into shape.

In concluding this chapter I suggest that modern, culturally under-developed hunter-gatherers, (after we eliminate intrusive cultural elements they have adopted from culturally more complex societies), have preserved a life-style, which in several respects ought to resemble that of prehistoric hunter-gatherers; and which, if compared in terms of stone-tool technology alone, is even below the cultural level achieved by some Homo habilis, of c. 2 million years ago.

Seen in a world-wide historical context, these hunter-gatherers, as well as their prehistoric forbears, appear to completely disprove the thesis held by many contemporary anthropologists that human culture is part and parcel of an evolutionary process universally applicable to all humankind. The fact that this cultural assessment turns out now to be highly suspect, also has a great bearing on cultural theories related to evolution. This is a subject which will be dealt with in more detail in PART II of this series of articles.

8. AN ANATOMY OF STONE-TOOLS

A study of the archaeological record of stone-tool making reveals a striking continuity in shapes and functions extending over millions of years, beginning with the simple pebble tools of A. afarensis and Homo habilis and ending with the refined products of the Upper Palaeolithics. It further seems that successive hominid species (apart from late Homo sapiens) were each initially associated with a specific tool type: A afarensis and Homo habilis with pebble-tools, Homo erectus with the Acheulian hand-axe complex, the Neanders with Mousterian assemblies, the Upper Palaeolithics with a blade technology, and Neolithics with polished stone tools.

The question which arises here is whether identical stages of stone-tool making arose independently in different parts of the world in the form of parallel developments, or whether each technical advance had its unique place of origin, spreading from there by physical contact either directly or indirectly, to other parts of the world?

As to pre-stone tool making Australopithecines (and some modern hunter-gatherers also), we can conjecture that they had little motivation to deliberately fashion stone-tools, since there was plenty of stone debris lying about to serve as knives and scrapers without their needing retouching. In its beginnings, tool-making may have consisted of occasionally striking some additional chips from a jagged stone to give it a more regular edge, for, as J. Gowlett observes (1984), nothing is sharper than a fresh edge.

However, such incipient tools can hardly be distinguished

from unworked stones. Comparable is Forde's description of contemporary Semang (Malaysian hunter-gatherers). He observed (1968), that although the Semang use stone-tools, these are very under-developed. 'For example, the splitting and scraping of wood is done with rough, shapeless stones, picked up at need and thrown away again'.

The oldest pebble tools so far recorded are from Hadar Ganda in Ethiopia, with a suggested dating of c. 2.6 million years. According to D. Johanson they are comparable to tools made by Homo habilis c. half a million years later at Olduvai, Omo, and Lake Turkana. Pebble tools were succeeded by hand-axe shaped implements. According to J. Gowlett (1984), 'the idea of working two opposite faces of a stone (a basic feature of the Acheulian hand-axe G.K.) can be traced right back to early Oldowan at Olduvai, where it is seen in discoids'.[1]

Nevertheless, the older forms of core-tools, flakes and scrapers continue to be produced throughout the Acheulian era, and on some sites they greatly outnumber hand-axes'. The more sophisticated Acheulian type hand-axe itself, resulted from a novel technique of stone-knapping. According to R. Leakey and D. Johanson, these latter tools appeared rather suddenly c. 1½ million years ago at Olduvai in association with the species Homo erectus. Over the following million or more years, the Acheulian hand-axe complex remained the predominant toolkit of hominids throughout the Old World.

R. Leakey has suggested that the Acheulian stone industry at Olduvai was the fountainhead from which other Acheulian sites derived their cultural capital. In R. Leakey's opinion (1981), 'The Acheulian industry continued, with steady refinements, right to the end of the sequence at Olduvai, and when some African hominids migrated north, they took their technology with them'. Acheulian hand-axe industries are known throughout the length and breadth of Africa, in the Middle East, in most of Europe and in the Indian sub-continent. Recent finds indicate an Acheulian technology in Mongolia and even in Korea (Gowlett, 1984). The latest hand-axe makers fall within the definition Homo sapiens.[2]

However, as already indicated, the emergence of the hand-

Figure 12. Member 5 Early Acheulian artefacts. Top, left to right: 2 cleavers on flakes with bulbs trimmed away and a core. Bottom, left to right: unifacial handaxe on a flake, bifacial handaxe, chopper. Bifacial handaxe is made on chert and all other pieces on quartzite.
From R. Dart: *Hominid Evolution: The Dart Symposium.*

axe did not lead to an abandonment of pebble tools. Almost a million years later core-tools, flakes and scrapers were still being used by Homo erectus pekinensis, but there were no hand-axes. In contrast, Homo erectus javanensis, although belonging to the same species, was found without stone tool association (Clark and Piggott, 1970). This latter find supports the previous conjecture that only a limited number of hominids within identical species made stone-tools.

Figure 13: Tools of the Moustrean industry: left, a stone core from which flakes were struck; centre, a side-scraper used for cleaning hides; right, a point, a tool which could have been used as a tip of an arrow or spear. These tools date to c. 100,000 years ago.

What has also already been noted is that chronologically the sequence of the Acheulian attributed to Homo erectus, proceeded deeply into the Homo sapiens era. There was no profound change in the Acheulian toolkit (which commenced c. 1½ million years ago) until c. 150,000 B.P. when it was superseded by the Neanders' Levallosian-Mousterian culture complex. At that time Homo sapiens was already c. 150,000 years old.

About the Mousterian (Mou.) technology, J. Gowlett cites the following details (1984). 'The Mou. toolkit is chiefly based on the use of flint-flakes about 4 – 7 cm. long. These are shaped into specialised tools by the process of retouch. In addition to the Typical Mou., and a variant which includes hand-axes, there are the Quina and Ferrassie types which are noted for a particular sort of scrapers, and the Denticulate Mou. with its "saw edged" tools. In the Middle East, the Mou. emerged out of the late Ach. sometimes by way of local variants. Also in the Middle East transitional finds between Neanders and Modern man have been claimed for sites at Mt. Carmel (Israel) and Djebel Qafzeh. Most Neander finds are associated with the Mou. A recent find at St. Cesaire, France, a very late Neander-phase (30,000 B.P.) is associated with an early Upper Palaeolithic phase, the Chattelperonian. It indicates that the Upper Palaeolithic blade technology could be mastered by the Neanders, thus indicating a transitional periods. By developing this specific blade technology the Upper Palaeolithics produced an entirely new arsenal of more refined tools as well as, adding implements of bones, antlers and ivory, and other more sophisticated artefacts'.

However, according to J. Gowlett, *a blade technology* had already appeared c. 100,000 years B.P. in the Middle East and in Africa but never reached great favour (except in Europe, where it became dominant). In Europe the Upper Palaeolithics heralded new peaks of achievement in stone and bone working c. 34,000 B.P., while in the Middle East a similar development is noticeable from c. 40,000 B.P. onwards.

Of special interest among the tool-types of this period, are the *Solutrean* ones (c. 19,000 B.C.). They are believed to have been made over a mere 2000 years period in France and Spain. They are manifest by the use of long narrow blades up to 30 cm. long, though the usual length is 8 – 10 cm., (the so-called *laurel* leaf points). Yet preceding this, cruder varieties existed in the Mousterian of Central and Eastern Europe. The technique used is called pressure (or invasive flaking and involves a very delicate craftsmanship. What is particularly notable is that laurel-leaf points have been found during the last few thousand years in late pre-Dynastic Egypt, and more remarkably still, in pre-Columbian North and South America (J. Gowlett, 1984).

Figure 14. A flint spear-head of the `laurel-leaf' type, dating c. 18,000 years ago. This particular style was restricted to a small area of western Europe.

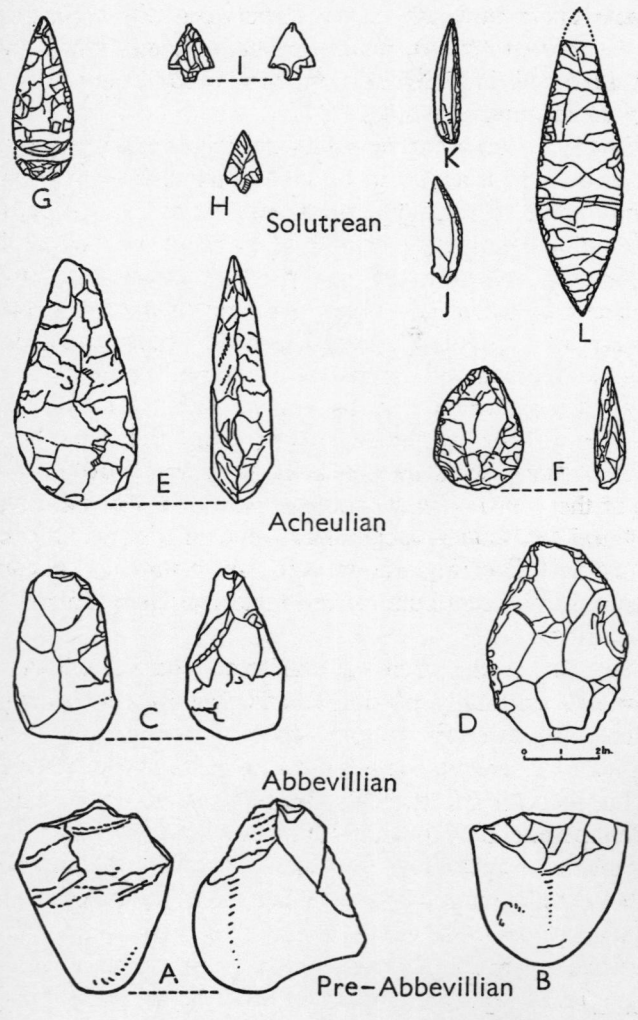

Solutrean

Acheulian

Abbevillian

Pre-Abbevillian

Figure 15. Tools assumed to have been particular to the periods referred to above.

Microliths (small pointed blades), used for spear and later for arrow points, seem to have appeared as early as 90,000 years ago in South Africa. They disappeared sometime later, only to reappear again in South Africa at between 20,000 and 10,000 B.P. J. Gowlett (1984), observes that it seems likely that the ideas involved in their manufacture were retained by some group, rather than reinvented.

Finally, of note are the rather crudely worked *edge-ground stone axes*, which appeared in an Australian-New Guinea orbit around 38,000 to c. 22,000 years ago. They seem to be unconnected with the finely ground and polished as well as hafted stone-axes which emerged in S.W. Asia around 7000 to 6000 B.C. The Australian-New Guinea tool seems undoubtedly representative of one of the rare cases of independent parallel development, although resemblances are rather cursory.

What conclusion can be drawn from a review of this confusing welter of different stone-tool varieties, types and technologies? Many seem to appear quite sporadically in different parts of the world – with parallel tool forms like the Solutrean type laurel-leaf blades, (resulting from a most intricate technique of stone-tool knapping, known as pressure flaking) appearing in the entirely different cultural and historical environments of the Americas.

Yet out of the seeming confusion and complexity there emerges a continuity of shapes and functions stretching over millions of years. In a close study we can hardly find any complex type without some indication of it having arisen from a simpler, preceding form. It also becomes obvious that truly independent parallel developments appear to be rare.

Only two apparently convincing cases of the independent parallel development of stone-tools come to mind, one concerns the pebble tools of A. afarensis, which show no known connection with the similar Oldowan tools of Homo habilis dated half a million years later (c. 2 million years B.P.). Also the former show no progression towards the Acheulian hand-axe technology, while the latter do.

The other case concerns ground and polished stone-axes. The first finds of fully ground and polished, hafted, axe-heads, dated between 7000 and 6000 B.C. were reported from several locations in the Fertile Crescent of South West Asia. (C. Coon, 1967). Since then, examples of edge ground (unpolished) stone axes, with some hafting evidence, have been found in an Australian-New Guinean orbit (Arnhem Land, North Australia c. 23,000 B.C. and Huon Peninsula, New Guinea, c. 38,000 B.C.) These tools resulting doubtlessly from independent developments, turned out to be roughly shaped stone-axes, with only the cutting edge ground, the rest unworked. Furthermore, these finds have so far remained isolated examples of any early edge-ground stone axe, without any evidence of further refinement, or of spreading over wider areas.

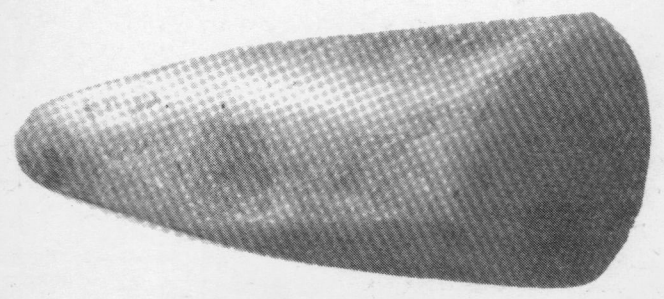

Figure 16. Neolithic polished axe.

In contrast the polished hafted axe of the Fertile Crescent spread almost immediately around the entire area followed by a relatively rapid world-wide distribution including the Americas. It may at first glance appear that the identical tools of pre-Columbian America (c. 1500 B.C.), are examples of independent parallel invention or development; in respect of both the polished stone-axe and the Solutrean-type laurel-leaf point. Yet it is exactly the identity of their refinement and the particularity of the historical time context in which they both appeared, which throws doubt on their independent origin in the Americas. One may therefore suggest that when correctly assembled and classified in sequence, the history of stone-tool making the world over, illustrated and described in books and periodicals and exhibited in collections and museums throughout the continents, can be fitted into a framework comparable to the anatomical transformations in the animal kingdom. In outline the process involved allows a comparison with the Darwinian thesis of 'descent with modification', leading within the realm of stone-tools to new genera, species, and varieties; with some species of stone-tools ending in blind alleys.[1] While the undertaking of such a systematic classification of stone tool developments would require a Darwinian patience and perseverance, it is important to point out that while animal kingdom evolutionary developments are biological, being based on genetical inheritance, no biological evolutionary nor any cultural evolutionary process within the kingdom of stone tools is suggested here.

The situation is strikingly underlined by the proposition tentatively advanced in this paper that stone tool making throughout the millions of years of the stone-age was the preserve of only a minority of culturally developing hominids. The majority of hominids although biologically identical with their stone tool making contemporaries, took little or no interest in stone tool-making, nor in most other cultural developments. It can therefore *not* be asserted that a minority of hominids (the stone-tool makers) were part and parcel of an evolutionary cultural process while the majority (the no stone-tool makers) were not. Finally, as a general rule, the archaeological record of stone tools conveys the impression that the majority of identical parallel developments in stone-tool technology throughout the world resulted from continuing developments, which in each case ought to be traceable to a common source. Independent parallel emergencies of identical stone-tool types, if they can be proved at all, appear to be rare exceptions.

9. COMPARATIVE BRAIN AND CULTURAL CURVES

THE BRAIN CURVE

Firstly, it must be noted that the projected brain curve D-I is based on brain size only, as there exists no valid denominator to determine the brain's functional value. Secondly, brain size has no direct relationship to brain quality, although in terms of overall hominid evolution a certain marginal relationship between brain size and cultural development may exist.

The brain curve plots hominid brain evolution (in terms of size), over a space of four million years. This is in accordance with D. Johanson's estimate (1982), that the hominid A. afarensis may reach back this far. Hence we commence our brain curve with the mean value of H. afarensis, which is c. 415 cc. (i.e., between 380 cc. and 450 cc.), a figure which tallies with the brain sizes of other Australopithecines. On the tail end of the curve we place the mean of present Homo sapiens, which is c. 1350 cc., a figure which has remained fairly constant throughout his almost 300,000 years of existence.

The brain curve stretches therefore between the mean values of the earliest known hominids and present day humans. The resulting increase in brain size over the period is seen as c. 1000 cc. In marking the intermediate stages of the projected curve and considering the 8 different diagrams of hominid descent and succession we find that some species branched off at certain evolutionary stages only to become extinct later; others again run parallel for some time only to share extinction, others again overlapped or merged with their successors. To solve the dilemma I have chosen as approximate sign-posts for intermediate stages, Homo habilis and Homo erectus, even though they may occupy these positions only temporarily.

It was still believed fairly recently that Homo erectus emerged about half a million years ago on the evolutionary scene including such well known types as Pithecanthropus, Sinanthropus, and the Steinheim and Swanscome fossils (the latter two are now classified as Homo sapiens). But since then several older Homo erectus fossils have been found, the oldest as Koobi Fora in N. Kenya. According to Johanson (1982): 'this was Richard Leakey's most significant find; an excellent Homo erectus skull dated $1\frac{1}{2}$ million years'. Johanson concluded that Homo sapiens evolved from some of the later erectus types between 400,000 and 100,000 years ago (Johanson, 1982, P.V. Tobias, 1983a).

The succession of the two species, Homo erectus and Homo sapiens (or rather their overlap or merger), at a mean value of c. 1350 cc. can be arbitrarily fixed on our brain curve at a point marking the date of 300,000 B.P., (although this point could alternate anywhere between 400,000 and 200,000 B.P.). From then on, i.e., 300,000 years ago, it can be assumed that the mean brain size of Homo sapiens (with some variations) remained constant up to the present. Therefore, the last 300,000 years of the brain curve can be drawn as a straight line, indicating a stagnation in brain development (at least in size) for the entire period.

One important deviation from the present brain curve must however be stressed, namely such varieties of Homo sapiens as the Neanderthalers, and later the Upper Palaeolithics, reached conspicuously higher average brain sizes than present Homo sapiens during a period of between c. 100,000 B.C., and 10,000 B.C. Although these diversions are omitted in our brain curve

75

they are separately commented upon. In spite of this omission it is hoped that the brain curve as it now stands, conveys a sufficiently acceptable picture of the general trend of human brain evolution over the last four million years, serving also as useful parameter when being contrasted with the cultural curve that follows.

THE CULTURAL CURVES (AS PROJECTED IN D-II, D-III, D-IV AND D-V)

First, it is emphasized that we are dealing here with two culturally distinct groups of hominids (even though they are biologically identical). The first group includes that minority of hominids projected in curve D-II, those that are *culturally developing*. The second group, projected in curve D-III (or rather line) forms the majority of pre-Neolithic hominids, which (although paralleling the former in brain potentials), have remained *culturally under-developed*. Their cultural status is symbolically drawn as a straight line expressing cultural stagnation. Its surviving remnants could be found until recently among culturally under-developed hunter-gatherers of our age.

However, even in the case of culturally developing hominids we find that initial cultural progress was tantalisingly slow. Paralleling the millions of years of human brain evolution with cultural progression we find that the comparison does not come up to expectations. For example a period of $2^{1}/_{2}$ million years (from 4 million years ago) was occupied successively by A. afarensis and Homo habilis, and in a possibly separate line of descent by A. boisei and A. robustus. All the visible cultural progress these hominids achieved in terms of stone-tool development (and we have no other measure) was a marginal improvement in pebble-tools, yet the average rise in brain size had been c. 400 cc. In other words, hominid cultural progress over $2^{1}/_{2}$ million years measured in stone-tool development was practically nil. When we reach Homo erectus and follow his biological evolution from $1^{1}/_{2}$ million to c. 300,000 years ago (the advent of Homo sapiens), we find a great increase in average brain size (from c.950 cc. to c.1350 cc.) which ought to

76

SYMBOLIC-DIAGRAMS

SHOWING THE CURVE OF HOMINID BRAIN EVOLUTION IN RELATION TO THEIR CULTURAL HISTORY – OVER 4 MILLION ys

A. = Australopithecus; H. = Homo; mys = millions of years; tys = thousands of years; c. = circa; cc = cubic cm; BP = Before Present.
All time periods and brain sizes are approximate.

D–I: HOMINID BRAIN CURVE

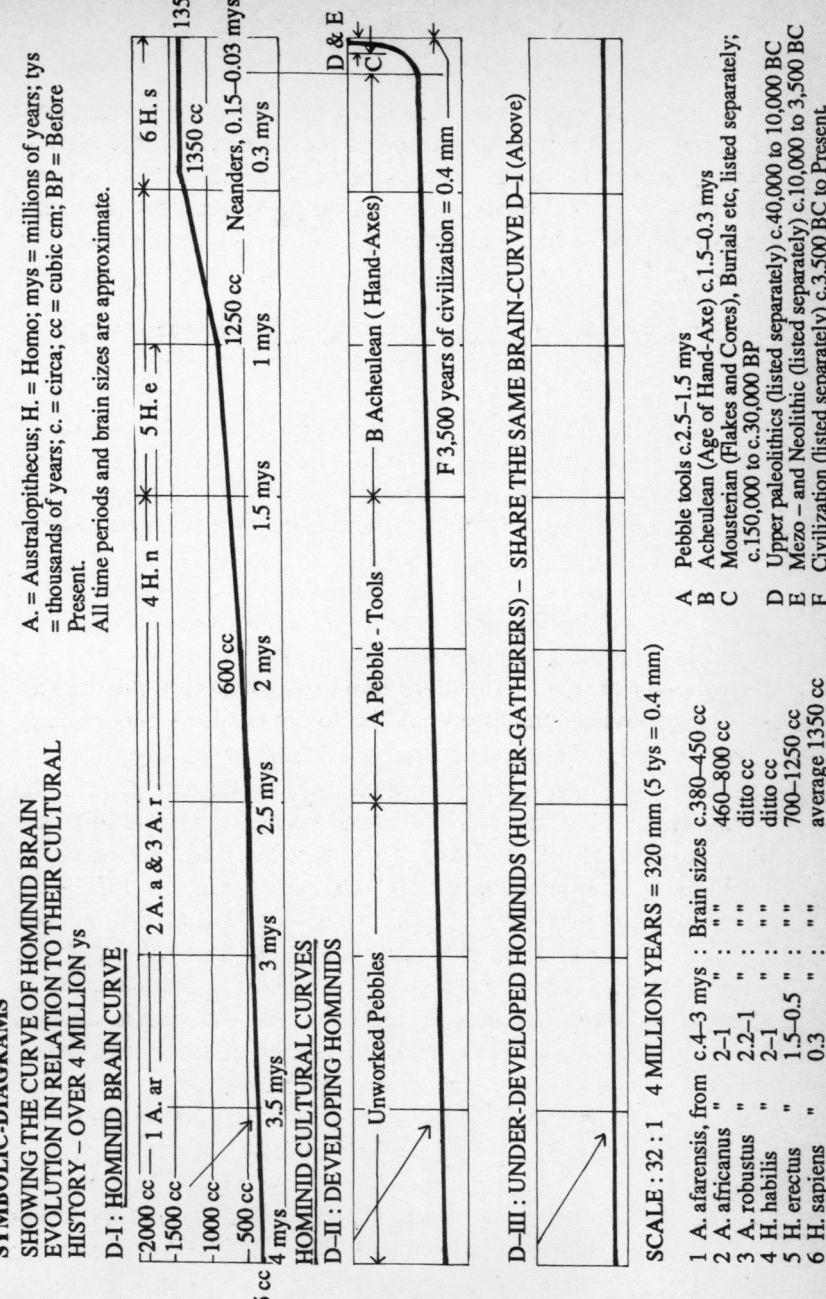

HOMINID CULTURAL CURVES
D–II: DEVELOPING HOMINIDS

D–III: UNDER-DEVELOPED HOMINIDS (HUNTER-GATHERERS) – SHARE THE SAME BRAIN-CURVE D–I (Above)

SCALE: 32:1   4 MILLION YEARS = 320 mm (5 tys = 0.4 mm)

A   Pebble tools c.2.5–1.5 mys
B   Acheulean (Age of Hand-Axe) c.1.5–0.3 mys
C   Mousterian (Flakes and Cores), Burials etc, listed separately; c.150,000 to c.30,000 BP
D   Upper paleolithics (listed separately) c.40,000 to 10,000 BC
E   Mezo – and Neolithic (listed separately) c.10,000 to 3,500 BC
F   Civilization (listed separately) c.3,500 BC to Present

1	A. afarensis,	from c.4–3 mys	Brain sizes	c.380–450 cc
2	A. africanus	" 2–1 "	"	460–800 cc
3	A. robustus	" 2.2–1 "	"	ditto cc
4	H. habilis	" 2–1 "	"	ditto cc
5	H. erectus	" 1.5–0.5 "	"	700–1250 cc
6	H. sapiens	" 0.3 "	"	average 1350 cc

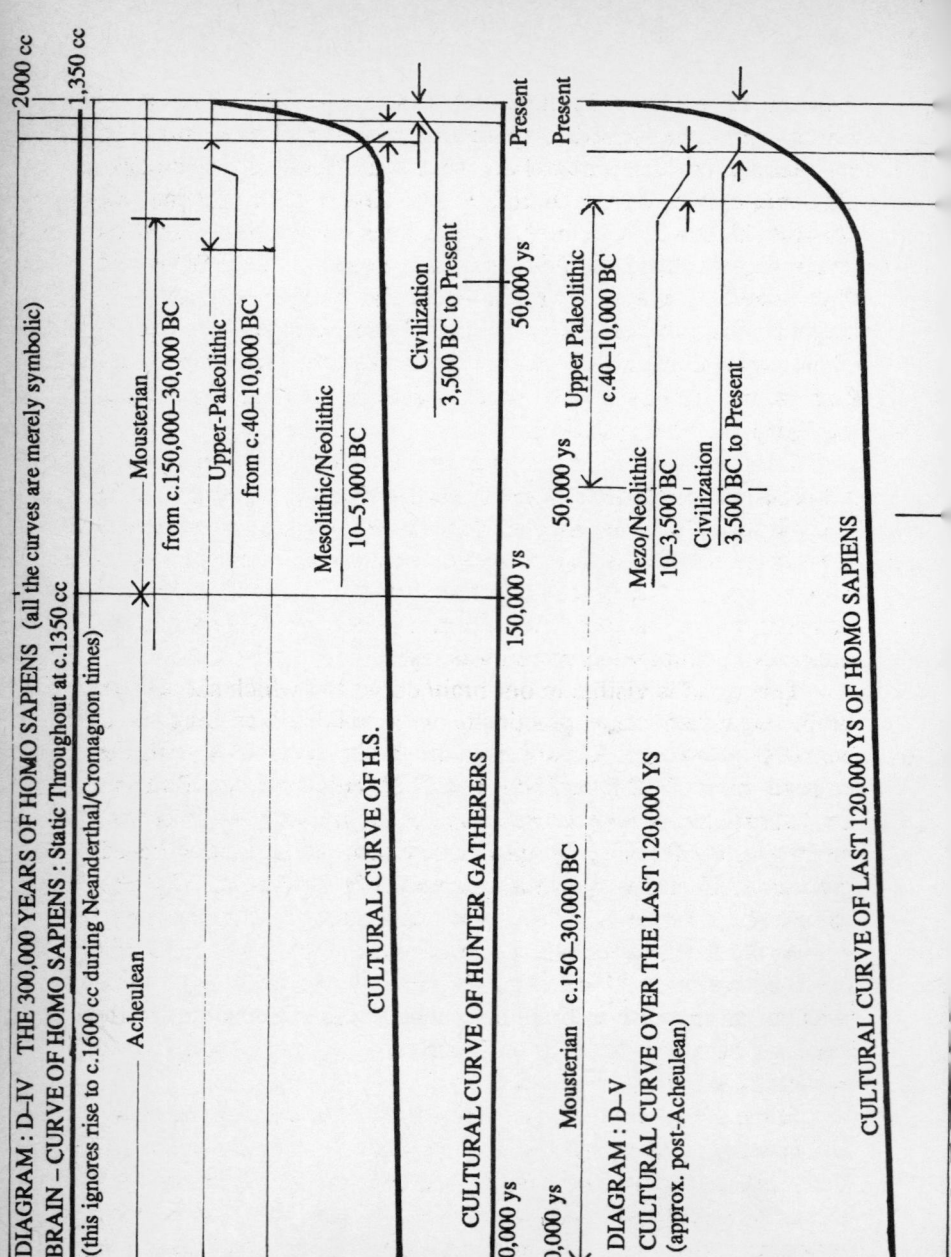

DIAGRAM : D-IV   THE 300,000 YEARS OF HOMO SAPIENS   (all the curves are merely symbolic)
BRAIN – CURVE OF HOMO SAPIENS : Static Throughout at c.1350 cc
(this ignores rise to c.1600 cc during Neanderthal/Cromagnon times)

2000 cc
1,350 cc

Acheulean

Mousterian
from c.150,000–30,000 BC

Upper-Paleolithic
from c.40–10,000 BC

Mesolithic/Neolithic
10–5,000 BC

Civilization
3,500 BC to Present

Present

CULTURAL CURVE OF H.S.

300,000 ys
150,000 ys   Mousterian   c.150–30,000 BC   150,000 ys

CULTURAL CURVE OF HUNTER GATHERERS

DIAGRAM : D-V
CULTURAL CURVE OVER THE LAST 120,000 YS
(approx. post-Acheulean)

50,000 ys   Upper Paleolithic
                   c.40–10,000 BC

Mezo/Neolithic
10–3,500 BC

Civilization
3,500 BC to Present

Present

50,000 ys

CULTURAL CURVE OF LAST 120,000 YS OF HOMO SAPIENS

78

indicate an increase in intelligence as well. Yet in terms of cultural progress (based on stone tools) we see no more than the refinement of the Acheulian hand-axe from more crudely produced tools. Again therefore, we find cultural stagnation, though this time on a higher level, over more than a million years. Commenting on this, Johanson writes (1982): 'Why did that culture (i.e. the Acheulian) and the Man who made it – stagnate for another million years? Homo erectus, it is fairly clear evolved practically not at all during the immense time'. Except, the present author likes to add, in his brain size when evolving into Homo sapiens.

The increase in brain size up to 1350 cc., between c. 500,000 and c. 300,000 years ago coincided approximately with the advent of Homo sapiens. Yet cultural stagnation prevailed for almost another 150,000 years more, until c. 150,000 years ago, when the Mousterian culture heralded a major cultural advance. From then on, and in spite of more or less stagnating brain sizes, cultural expansion was rapid.

This trend is visible in our brain curve D-I which shows that brain expansion came practically to a standstill as long as c. 300,000 years ago. Contrasting the brain curve D-I with the cultural curve D-II (and D-IV and D-V, enlarged), we find that the latter made a steep ascent towards the tail end of the period, ending in the dizzying heights of our own, scientifically based, modern civilization. But this progress only applies to culturally developing hominids, while their culturally under-developed counterparts remained until recently, on a cultural level not much above that of Homo habilis. Here the question arises: if it was not an increase in brain size, which was responsible for the sudden advance of the culturally developing section of humanity, what was the cause?

Some observers have maintained that it was an evolutionary increase in the brains' intellectual qualities (quite independent of size) and not brain size, which was, and still is, responsible for humanity's cultural rise. At a first glance this assumption appears reasonable, and one can even agree that over the enormous period of millions of years which preceded the advent of agriculture and civilization, a marginal increase in brain quality relative to size, was indeed responsible for cultural advances. But one sees no biological evolutionary factors at work, which could have increased the brain's intellectual potentials, especially during later human history, which experienced the dramatic cultural expansion of the Neolithic period and of Civilization. The reasons for this have been examined in Chapter 6 – 'The Brain's Intellectual Qualities'.

Furthermore, seen in this context, the question why such an increase in brain qualities should only apply to culturally developing hominids, while eluding their culturally stagnant biological equals is left unexplained.

On the other hand, as suggested here, it can be seen that cultural progress is not generally due to the direct influence of increased intelligence, but is mainly based on the accumulation of knowledge and experience and its transmission. This is followed again by the addition of further knowledge acquired by future generations in a perpetuum-mobile fashion. This principle of cultural progress is particularly prominent in our own modern world where we can observe that as knowledge broadens, the possibilities of further growth increase in almost geometrical progression. In short, cultural progress can be self-generating, it all depends on prevailing opportunities as well as on the will, motivation and inter-action, of the individuals concerned.

10. A CULTURAL ASSESSMENT OF HOMO SAPIENS

Following a re-classification of fossils formerly listed under Homo erectus, latest estimates put the emergence of Homo sapiens at between 400,000 and 200,000 years B.P., suggesting a medium of 300,000 years B.P. They include finds at Verteszollos, Hungary; Swanscombe, England; and Steinheim,

Germany. The Verteszollos fossils have been renamed Homo sapiens paleo-hungaricus, with an estimated age of 200,000 years and a mean brain size of c. 1400 cc. This compares with the contemporary Homo sapiens brain of 1350 cc. (Bray/Trump, 1970; J. Campbell, 1983). Also of interest is the Swanscombe fossil, with an estimated age range of between 300,000 and 200,000 years, and a female brain size given as 1325 cc. (v. Bonin, 1963), which indicates a mean between male and female of 1400 cc., being well above present brain averages.

As to the achievements of culturally developing Homo sapiens, in terms of stone-tool development, to the best of our knowledge during his first 150,000 years (between 300,000 and 150,000 B.P.), they hardly exceeded the cultural achievements of their evolutionary predecessors Homo erectus. As Bray/Trump have pointed out (1970), the tools associated with Homo sapiens paleo-hungaricus (age c. 200,000 years), include small choppers made from pebbles and various flake-tools. One can observe that both resemble the tools found at Bed II at Olduvai in E. Africa, which are a million years older. In Europe, hungaricus shows affinities with Clactonian tool types. In comparison, the earlier Swanscombe fossil was found with Middle Acheulian hand-axes, and at a lower level with Clactonian-type tools. Thus for c. 150,000 years or more, up to the advent of the Mousterian culture of the Neanders (at between c. 150,000 and 30,000 B.P.), Homo sapiens stagnated at the Acheulian level of culture already acquired a million years earlier by preceding Homo erectus. This in spite of the fact that at this distant age, Homo sapiens had already reached the average brain size of present humans. A cultural advance beyond the Acheulian was only achieved when the Neanders (now considered a sub-species, or variety of H.S.), introduced the Mousterian culture.

In an assessment of the latter's physique D. Johanson writes (1982), 'I consider Neanderthal con-specific with Sapiens. One hears talk about putting him in a business suit and turning him loose in the subway. It is true one could do it, and he would never be noticed'. What is more, according to W.W. Howell and E. Trinkaus (1980), their average brain size was 1600 cc. well above that of modern man.

81

Yet during their c. 120,000 years of existence, (from 150,000 to 30,000 B.P.) the Neanders could not pride themselves of any dramatic cultural advance comparable with later Neolithic achievements. Some insight into their cultural limitations has been provided by Clark/Piggott (1979), who point to their apparent lack of concern with personal decorations, or art, and the total absence of perforated animal teeth, which later became the commonest of all ornaments worn by prehistoric hunters. Although the Neanders lived frequently in caves, the total absence of any cave-art is another remarkable omission.

The Upper Palaeolithics who followed the Neanders biologically and culturally, were a younger version of Homo sapiens, preceding contemporary humans. Though producing a wealth of sophisticated artefacts and a greatly admired cave-art, they were nevertheless culturally below their Neolithic successors. Thus, although they occupied large parts of the Old World for c. 30,000 years (c. 40,000 to 10,000 B.C.) and their average brain size is assessed by some authorities at 1600 cc. (Thomas 1969 – *see under* M. Day), they never achieved the late Neolithic and post-Neolithic feats of later Homo sapiens – culminating in food-production and civilization, all this occurring in a period of hardly 7000 years, roughly between c. 10,000 to 3000 B.C.

In considering the specific achievements of culturally developing Homo sapiens, two factors need stressing. One, that his life-span covers c. 300,000 years, and two, that throughout this period average brain sizes remained fairly constant, except during Neander and Upper Palaeolithic times when they showed a conspicuous elevation, which subsequently reverted back to previous averages. Furthermore, no conclusive evidence has so far been produced to show that throughout this latter period (from c. 10,000 B.C. onwards to the present) the functional, or intellectual, value of the sapiens' brain increased although such a possibility is not entirely excluded.

The c. 300,000 years of Homo sapiens life-span preceding food-production, can perhaps be divided into c. 15,000 generations of 20 years each. With each generation assessed at 10 million people (see J. Campbell, 1983). Accepting this figure we can arrive at a total world population of c. 7½ billion over this period of 300,000 years. In accordance with previous observations (*see* Chapter 7) only a small part of this huge population can have taken part in cultural developments, while the rest persisted on the level of culturally under-developed, non stone-tool making hunter-gatherers, though as a rule using unworked stones.

The Meso-Neolithic period (c. 10,000 to 3,500 B.C.), which towards its end harboured the first stirrings of civilization, and thus forms the sequence preceding civilization, spans c. 6500 years, or 325 generations. By adhering to a world population rota of 10 million per generation, we obtain a total Homo sapiens population for this latter period, lasting c. 6500 years, of 3250 millions. A scrutiny of agricultural beginnings world-wide, shows that only a small minority of these Homo sapiens could have initially engaged in food-production, while the remaining billions remained food-gatherers and hunters, some of them up to the present time.

Finally, the last developmental period to be reviewed is a span of a mere 200 years (not more than 10 generations) between c. 3300 and c. 3100 B.C. marking the almost simultaneous unfolding of the Sumerian and ancient Egyptian civilizations, both arising from an agricultural base. This sudden cultural explosion, was restricted to two relatively small riverine areas, a thousand miles apart. Indications are that everything that came after, was largely a blooming of the seeds that these two civilizations had planted earlier on, with one of them being the catalyst of the other.

Inquiring into the origins of food-production, we have to ask (as in the case of stone-tools), whether agriculture arose independently in many parts of the world or whether its beginnings are traceable to common sources of origin. J. Gowlett, who inclines towards the acceptance of many independent origins of agriculture nevertheless, expresses surprise at the almost simultaneous world-wide emergence of agriculture. He writes (1984): 'There is not much evidence of domestication before 10,000 years ago, but by 7000 years ago cultivated crops and domesticated animals began to appear over large areas of the world, including America. All this did not come overnight, but in relation to two million years of hunting and gathering, the greatest ever alteration of economy came amazingly suddenly'.

Considering *the special case of cereal cultivation*, it involves the selection of the right seeds from hundreds of wild grasses, and the growing of them in bulk, an altogether hazardous enterprise needing much experimentation. Once successful around 7000 B.C. on the fringes of the Fertile Crescent of S.W. Asia, cereal cultivation, soon spread to almost everywhere. Yet throughout the entire period preceding 7000 B.C. (or at most 10,000 B.C.) there was no known cereal cultivation anywhere in the world. In the Far East early cultivation of rice in China dates back to c. 5000 B.C., while earlier claims for Thailand (c. 6800 B.C. – Spirit Cave), have remained dubious. In Africa earliest cereal cultivation is reported from the Fayum Oasis dating back to 5200 B.C. (Trigger, 1983). In the Americas, earliest maize cultivation date back to c. 5000 B.C. in Mexico (Tehuacan Valley). In Europe earliest traces of cultivation have been found in Cyprus, dated c. 6100 B.C. and in Thessaly (Greece), dated c. 5500 B.C. The most significant omission from this list is the continent of Australia, where cereal growing had to await modern European colonization.

What all these dates show is that the world's early cereal cultivation fell within a time range of hardly 2000 years (i.e., from c. 7000 – 5000 B.C.). Yet preceding this, Homo sapiens, throughout his c. 300,000 years (minus 10,000 years) pre-agricultural history, never succeeded in cultivating cereals anywhere (although possibly there were abortive attempts). And yet during this huge expanse of time there must have occurred numerous occasions when climatic and soil conditions, and the presence of suitable grass-seeds must have favoured cereal cultivation. For example, J. Gowlett (1984) points out that just over 120,000 years ago, for about 10,000 years, the climate in most of the world was very similar to that of today, in land, sea, and vegetation. Yet there was no sudden development towards agriculture and civilization.

In view of this the following proposition stands to reason. Presuming that during the 300,000 years of Homo sapiens existence (preceding agriculture) there was, arbitrarily, at least one favourable occasion every hundred years to grow cereals, there could have been at least 3000 such occasions. Yet, as far as we know, not one such opportunity was utilised. The assumption therefore, that the world's cereal cultivation started up almost simultaneously and independently in many widely separated areas of the world within a narrow time span of 2000 years, despite the fact that during the preceding c. 300,000 (minus 10,000 years) of Homo sapiens existence, absolutely nothing of the kind occurred, is very tenuous.

Many years ago Gordon Childe highlighted this situation when he wrote (1966) 'It must not be imagined that at a given moment in the world's history a trumpet was blown in heaven, and every hunter from China to Peru thereupon flung away his weapons and traps and started planting wheat or rice and breeding pigs, sheep and turkeys'.[1]

In contrast, J. Gowlett has tried to explain why many archaeologists accept independent agricultural origins. He points out that modern humans before taking to agriculture, gradually had accumulated similar levels of cultural experience, had encountered similar problems and had affected similar adaptations. But has this really been the case? The archaeological record shows otherwise.

Before agriculture took hold the world was exclusively populated by hunter-gatherers, the majority of whom had never advanced to the alleged level of cultural experience (mentioned by Gowlett), which ought to have led them almost automatically into agricultural pursuits; and this, although throughout hundreds of thousands of years they had encountered similar foraging problems and lived in the same environment as their culturally more advanced contemporaries, while biologically they stood all on the same Homo sapiens level.

Furthermore, the theory claiming an almost automatic progress towards agriculture, is contradicted by the Australian experience. According to Gowlett himself (1984), one group of South East Asian hominids crossed into Australia (via New Guinea) as early as 70,000 to 60,000 years ago, while another followed c. 20,000 years later. Neither group ever practised agriculture. Yet the prevailing conditions in Australia ought to have favoured such a development, as, along with other cultural elements, Gowlett reports the discovery of grinding stones dated c. 15,000 B.P., commenting that their presence suggest the exploitation of seeds and their grinding.

In both the Old World and the New the presence of grindstones and querns, indicating the collection of wild growing grains and their grinding into flour, (dating in the Old World well back over 200,000 years (Carter: 1973a)), has long been considered as a prelude to the deliberate cultivation of cereals (i.e. agriculture). In Australia such grain collecting and grinding is also evidenced but led to no further development. When grain cultivation was eventually introduced into Australia in the wake of European colonization about two hundred years ago, the continent became one of the world's leading grain producers.

The conclusion follows, that when all the evidence for and against the independent parallel emergence of agricultural beginnings (especially for grain cultivation) is considered, the indications for a single origin followed by world wide spread from this source far outweigh anything advanced in favour of multiple independent origins.[2]

11. THE CASE OF EARLY CIVILIZATION

As indicated in previous chapters under 'Post Acheulian Cultures', the term civilization as used here refers to those more complex societies known as 'Urban Literate', typified by the two earliest examples, Sumer and ancient Egypt. Both arose almost concurrently against a background of big river irrigative agriculture, between c. 3300 and 3100 B.C., a span of a mere 200 years. In this short period both civilizations appear to have displayed many of the basic traits which led to their later splendour. Their formative stages dating back to perhaps 4000 B.C. and before are still only vaguely discernible, and although present evidence favours Sumer as having been the earlier civilization there are indications that Egyptian priority cannot be ruled out.

The essential accomplishments which separate these two early civilizations from preceding less complex societies, include the use of writing, the first recorded emergence of kings and gods (secular and divine), organized religion and its priesthood, large cities with thousands of inhabitants, monumental edifices, including temples, palaces and pyramids, and in Egypt, the early use of a calendar. It can be presumed that the remains of many ancient Egyptian cities lay still buried under the Nile valleys alluvium.

However, the appearance of many of these traits was not uniform in the two civilizations, neither chronologically nor in the sharing of common elements. Furthermore, in the course of time each civilization developed its own individual character. Yet, it is unlikely that such a cluster of distinct cultural elements held in common, could have arisen independently of each other, either singly or in combination, during the brief time these two civilizations reached prominence. Geographically, they lay about a thousand miles apart and it is notable that a depiction of Sumerian-type boats in pre-Dynastic Egypt, bears witness that inter-communication between the two existed since early times. J. Gowlett (1984) has observed that writing appeared at about the same time (between 3100 and 3000 B.C.), both in Mesopotamia and ancient Egypt. Since it appeared in Egypt, seemingly without any sign of preceding development, some authorities have suggested that the concept may have been imported from Mesopotamia. Latest research has shown that hieroglyphic writing, architecture as well as the monarchial institution in Nubia predated ancient Egypt by 200 years. (See Bruce Williams, 'The Lost Pharaohs of Nubia', in Ivan Van Sertima, ed., Nile Valley Civilizations [Journal of African Civilizations, New Jersey, 1985]. (Ed.)) There are however strong indications (detailed in Part IV, Volume II) that it could well have been the reverse.

Only a few hundred years later similar civilizations arose in India and China, and like their predecessors in Sumer and Egypt, they were situated in big river valleys, i.e., Indus and the Hoangho. Like their Sumerian and Egyptian antecedents, both India and China had early scripts, though the Indian script has so far defied decipherment. J. Gowlett says that the fact that writing appears several hundred years later in India and China than in Mesopotamia suggests that the inspiration for it came to them from this source.

These four Old World civilizations were all distinguished by large urban settlements, some of them still awaiting excavation. The architecture of pyramidal structures in China resembles that of the step-pyramids of the Sumerian ziggurats which again may go back to the ancient Egyptian step-pyramid of pharaoh Zoser of the III Dynasty. More remarkable is that similar step-pyramids are a prominent feature of Pre-Columbian American civilizations. In fact, in all early civilizations with the exception (so far) of India, we find an early presence of gods and kings and organized religion administered by a priestly class. In each case (again in India they are noted later) we find whole city states or nations ruled over by powerful kings, some of them worshipped as gods in their lifetime. These often formed dynasties, perpetuated by hereditary succession, the most prominent examples being the Pharaohs of Egypt ('Sons of the Sun' from the V Dynasty onwards), the Sons of Heaven in China, and the Inca ruler in Peru, claiming to be a 'Son of the Sun', and the Mikados of Japan, reputed to have descended from the sun goddess Amaterasu; they were worshipped as 'Living Gods' into modern times.

It is now generally conceded that there were many links between the Sumerian, Indian and Chinese civilizations, just as there were striking similarities between Sumer and Egypt. This is hardly surprising as for thousands of years before their emergence we find evidence of the movements of people and of trade covering enormous distances. For example, identical Venus-figurines of the lower Palaeolithic Gravettian culture (between 30,000 and 25,000 B.C.) have been identified at distances c. 3200 km. apart, from the foothills of the Pyrenees in Spain to the area of the lower Don in S. Russia. Cave art of a Magdalenian pattern (well before 10,000 B.C.), comparable in style, has been evidenced 4000 km. apart, at the Dordogne in France and in the S. Urals (Clarke/Piggott, 1970). More recent trading links have been mentioned by J. Gowlett (1984), for the period between c. 7000 and 5000 B.C. In such goods as sea-shells from the Indian Ocean to Mergarah (an outpost of the Indus Civilization) c. 800 km. to the north, and of lapis-lazuli from Badakshan in Central Asia to both, Mergarah 1000 km. to the south and via Afghanistan to Mesopotamia, a distance of 2500 km. A lively trade in obsidian, from the Lake Van area in Anatolia to both; S. Mesopotamia and to Palestine is also recorded.

In view of these facts, the postulation by some adherents of the theory of independent cultural development, namely that early civilizations, despite sharing many identical features, were in each case the isolated creations of their local inhabitants, appears no longer valid.

The manner in which this process of independent isolated parallel development is presumed to have occurred has been elucidated by Glyn Daniel, a leading exponent. He reasoned (1971) that 'seven societies in seven different ways trod the paths that led to civilization', basing his proposition on ideas earlier advanced by Kroeber and Caldwell. Kroeber had written (1940) 'We must consider that civilization is an inevitable response to laws governing the growth of culture and controlling the man-culture relationship'. And Caldwell (1966): 'Perhaps there is only a finite number of social and historical processes behind the events of history'. Daniel concluded (1971): 'I believe that an interpretation of the origin of civilization in terms of multilinear evolution (i.e., conforming with the ideas of Kroeber and Caldwell – G.K.), is in accordance with the archaeological facts as known to us'.

In the spirit of modern scientific enquiry, this deterministic approach to human history does not conform with archaeological facts as Daniel maintains. Under the conditions outlined by Daniel and Gowlett, two of the most advanced pre-civilized societies in the Near East, Jericho in Palestine, c. 8800 to c. 6000 B.C., and Čatal Hüyük in Anatolia c. 6750 B.C. and after, should have developed into fully fledged civilizations. Both went through the stages of a food-collecting economy, leading eventually to mixed farming and pottery making, with Čatal Hüyük even developing irrigative agriculture. Both these sites developed into large settlements, with many examples of artistic expressions and with Čatal Hüyük eventually occupying an area four times the size of Jericho.

However, neither of them erected *monumental temples or palaces*.[1] There is no evidence of any hierarchical structure of government headed by kings, no evidence of male gods and organized religion.[2] Neither of them used writing or a calendar. In fact Jericho on its own account never reached a higher level of culture akin to civilization, while Čatal Hüyük petered out of history and left nothing but ruins, recalling a Neolithic type of advanced farming society.[3]

In contrast with the favourable conditions prevailing at Jericho and Čatal Hüyük , Sumerian civilization established itself on what was originally a swampy wasteland without any trace of preceding cultural development, going much beyond the level of reed-hut fishing villages, presumed to have resembled those of contemporary Marsh-Arabs. This in an area not only devoid of wood, but also of stone and metals. It was in such a precarious environment that Sumerian civilization began, with Eridu (reputed to be the first city in the world) apparently establishing a tenuous foothold on an elevated sand-dune adjoining the Persian Gulf.[4]

The physical preconditions of the area where the first American civilization, that of the Olmecs, became established, c. 1200 B.C. (M. Coe, 1968), appear to have been equally unpromising. Coe writes that 'the abruptness of its appearance at the hot coastal plain of Southern Vera Cruz has no convincing explanation at the present moment'. A much later writer, Stuart Fiedel, (1987), comments that 'Much work remains to be done before we can fully understand why Olmec civilization should have arisen so precociously in a seemingly inhospitable environment'. And Jacques Soustelle, writing on the origin of the Olmecs (1985), points out that 'There is no evidence of "formative" evolution, a gradual maturation over several centuries. This indeed constitutes the very head of the Olmec mystery ... the astonishing spectacle of a civilization that gives the impression of suddenly springing up in all its originality from an undifferentiated background of peasant culture'. Soustelle concludes: 'We are naturally left to ponder the question whether this leap was not due to exterior influences?'

In this respect the finding of R.A. Jairazbhoy, who has traced Olmec origins to ancient Egyptian intrusion, are most revealing. Jairazbhoy (1974) shows the presence of ancient Egyptian parallels in Olmec Mexico from the time of Rameses III onwards. These include many identical replications of Egyptian gods, some Egyptian hieroglyphs, and a great deal more.

These few instances of factual evidence cast serious doubt on the validity of the multilinear evolutionary approach, which pretends to postulate the independent, isolated origins of the early civilizations in both the Old World and the New.

What then is the alternative?

Chapter 8: 'An Anatomy of Stone-Tools' presented a coherent case for a continuing development of stone-tool technology, showing the dissemination of specific tool-types from common sources of origin to widely separated parts of the world. We can propose that a similar process of spread from common origins predominates and explains the presence of other cultural parallels the world over, beginning with the Old Stone Age and ending with 'Modern Civilization'. Extensive supportive evidence will be submitted in Volume II of this work.

12. THE CULTURAL EPOCHS CHART

The process of cultural growth and spread is graphically shown in the attached chart, which arbitrarily divides the world's cultural output into six broadly based cultural epochs. However, the picture must be considered volatile, with a possible overlap of some cultural elements between historical epochs, as new archaeological discoveries are likely to cause changes within and between the different epochs. One instance of this which occurred after the chart had been completed for this manuscript, is the Neanderthal presence in Epoch 3, originally fixed between 120,000 and 50,000 years B.P. New evidence has now widened that range to between 150,000 and 30,000 B.P.

The chart shows that few or none of the achievements listed in any one epoch appear in any of the preceding epochs. For instance, none of the achievements of Epoch 6 are present in Epochs 5 through 1. The chart further illustrates that few or none of the essential cultural elements listed displays any known independent parallel presence or origin in any preceding epoch. *Each succeeding epoch's achievements are largely based on the accumulated stock of knowledge and experience of each preceding epoch, indicating a continuous cultural development from one epoch to the next.* Also many of the elements of the first five epochs still appear in Epoch 6, illustrating their persistence in the face of millions of years of cultural progression.

At the same time there is in each epoch a geographical dispersal of cultural elements. This is not indicated in the chart, though being detailed to some extent in the preceding the Chapter 5. It is shown there that while pebble tools spread over a wide area for two million years, the Acheulian hand-axe was developed in only one specific place, becoming the precursor of a new cultural epoch, 'The Acheulian'. This was followed by a wide dispersal of the hand-axe complex with many local refinements, until the Neanders introduced the Mousterian innovations and widened the field of stone-age technology. This was again followed by a specific Mousterian spread over a wider area, and so forth. In short, all cultural epochs can be shown to be historically related indicating a continuing cultural development.

The essential fact which emerges is that *all* cultural epochs appear to be historically related, both by direct and indirect contact, involving the principles of continuity and diffusion, though the process may be interspersed with rare examples of independent parallel developments.

The Cultural Epoch chart allows us to make another interesting deduction. In comparing the cultural output of Epoch 1 with that of Epoch 6, we find that it took perhaps 60,000 generations to create and persist with the meagre pebble-tool (seen as a simile, an elephant begetting a mouse). On the other hand, the mere 75 generations of Epoch 6, in only one eight thousandth (1:8000) part of the time of Epoch 1, produced a veritable colossus in cultural achievements (now a mouse producing an elephant). Finally we have the example not listed in the chart, of the culturally stagnant ultra-primitive hunter-gatherers (some of whom have survived into modern times). Their unbroken cultural history of 2½ million years or more, equalling about 125,000 generations, has, in terms of stone tool technology produced hardly more than pebble tools (comparably seen - as illustrated below - it is a mastodon producing a mite).

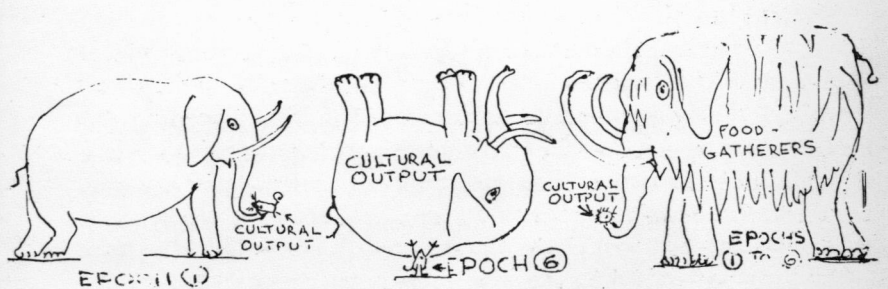

Figure 17. Elephants representing cultural epochs.

93

What these examples indicate is that it is not the direct influence of intelligence, or the number of generations which promote cultural growth. It is rather, a stock of accumulated knowledge and experience, and its transmission to future generations, which, circumstances permitting, leads to further advances. Furthermore, the presence of similar or identical cultural elements being found in widely dispersed parts of the world seems best explained by their derivation from common sources of origin.

CULTURAL EPOCHS CHART

Epochs 1–6: Their Growth per number of Generations, at 20 years per Generation. (The figure of 20 is arbitrary and may vary between 15–22. Please read chart from bottom up).

Early Old World Civilizations

4000 B.C. to 2300 B.C.

Big river irrigation, first observance of kings and gods (secular and divine), organised religion and priesthoods, erection of monumental buildings like temples, palaces and pyramids, a calendar, the use of writing, use of precious and semi-precious metals and stones, metallurgy, alloys like bronze, rudiments of mathematics and astronomy, an administrative bureaucracy, cities of thousands of inhabitants, etc.

Epoch 6 1,500 ys = 75 generations

Meso-Neolithic 10,000 B.C. to 4000 B.C.

Use of obsidian, copper, bitumen, sickles, grindstones and querns, agriculture and stock-rearing, small scale irrigation, spinning and weaving, mud-bricks, solid housing, extensive villages, elaborate burials, ground and polished (hafted) hand-axes, pottery, etc.

Epoch 5 6000 ys = 300 generations

Upper Palaeolithic 50,000 B.C. to 10,000 B.C.

Use of bone, antlers, ivory for tools and artefacts, stone and bone tips for spears and arrows, barbed harpoons, fishing tackle, animal and human figurines, cave-art, etc.

Epoch 4 40,000 ys = 2000 generations

Mousterian 120,000 to 50,000 B.C. (now revised: 150,000 to 30,000)

Flakes and cores of great variety, human burials, animal skins for cloths and shelters, etc.

Epoch 3 80,000 ys = 4000 generations

Acheulian 1.5 million to 120,000 yrs ago (possibly earlier)

Hand-axes

Epoch 2 1,380,000 ys = 69,000 generations

Lower Palaeolithic Pebble tools: 2.5 to 1.5 million years ago (but possibly earlier)

Epoch 1 1,000,000 ys = 50,000 generations

Observe the relative length in years of each Epoch, as we advance towards the Present. The amplitude of cultural creativeness (or output) increases by leaps and bounds (except between Epochs 1 and 2), while the time sequence projecting them shrinks dramatically in inverse proportion.

13. APPENDIX

The following is an extract from Chapter 14: The Role of Reason, from *Homo Sapiens in Decline* (G. Kraus, 1973).

The satisfaction of instincts, which are primary urges, depends on the aid of sensory perception. When these activities of the senses are analyzed, their coordination represents the phenomenon which we call the 'mental process', consisting of our powers of thinking or reasoning.

How do sense organs function? It can be presumed that an original primitive, discriminative sensitivity towards nourishment must have been the precursor of the sense of taste. In the same relationship stands light to vision, sound to hearing, pressure and other skin irritants to touch, and odours to smell. There exists also senses, like the echo sense in bats, or a time sense in birds and fish, which are orientated towards the sun and are outside the scope of normal human sensory perception.

The feeling of pain is of extraordinary importance for an individual's survival. Without it individuals would recklessly plunge into dangers, injuries would not be noticed, and even the loss of whole limbs would go unnoticed.

The senses of taste and smell are also influenced by pleasurable or distasteful reactions. The sexual act, for example, is accompanied by one of the most powerfully pleasurable sensations. On the other hand, the senses of vision and hearing are not generally guided by pleasure or displeasure, but human experience shows that visual and auditory tastes can be acquired and cultivated.

How is the mental process accomplished? To be of any use, senses must be able to discriminate between perceptions of different intensity. But this is only possible if sensory perceptions are separated in time. The bridging of this time-gap requires the retention and storage of sense impressions, or, in other words, the possession of a memory. Further, the comparison and evaluation of differing sense impressions, linked as they are by memory, amounts to the capacity of thinking or reasoning. It can therefore be asserted that even the most primitive form of sensory perception presupposes the possession of a memory and the capacity of thinking. Sensory perception existing without memory would be of no practical use whatsoever to any kind of living organism.

Some of the most primitive organisms, such as bacteria, viruses, and protozoa, exhibit traces of sensitivity, going beyond automatic reflex action. All these primitive life-forms must, therefore, possess memory, and though it may sound far-fetched, they must also be capable of thought. Such lowly organisms possess, of course, nothing like a brain. But they must inevitably possess some primitive nerve centre as the brain's forerunner, capable of associating and utilizing sense impressions. Thinking and memory therefore do not necessarily require a complicated organ like the brain.

Writers such as E. Hering believe that all organisms have memory, in as much as the action of a stimulus on protoplasm always leaves traces which influence further response. In this sense, the term learning may be extended to the simplest types of behaviour changes through stimulation, as in plants and protozoans. In the words of the 1961 edition of *Encyclopaedia Britannica*: 'If mind be granted to the higher vertebrates, the argument from the observed continuity in mode of behaviour indicates that it must be granted to the lower vertebrates and indeed to all animals including the protozoa. No distinction, moreover, can be made between the protozoa and the protophyta'.[1]

Even such a lowly organism as a virus, then, may be endowed with the rudiments of thinking. Now, viruses are generally so small that they pass the finest bacterial filters (bacteria themselves were once thought to be the smallest entities capable of independent life), but some of them carry in their chromosomes as many as six or seven thousand genetic determinants. The question is, why should such an utterly tiny organism as a virus carry so many thousands of genetic determinants?[2] The answer can only be that natural selection, considering the intense competition which must prevail amongst rapidly reproducing viruses, would not have tolerated the accumulation of so many thousands of genes unless they had been beneficial for survival. We must, therefore, assume that the thousands of genes of a virus control the thousands of different living processes that are necessary to keep it alive, amongst them in all probability genes controlling sensibilities, memory, and other aspects of mental action.

It should eventually become possible to locate more and more genes in the germ cells of animals and determine their functions. We may even predict that it will eventually be found that certain of the genetic determinants controlling nervous reactions, sensitivity, thought processes, and memory, in animals as well as in man, are already present in viruses and in bacteria.

It may even be discovered that the genetic system of a virus is more subtly balanced than that of man. The reason is that their rapid increase subjects them to an immeasurably more intense process of natural selection than the slower-breeding animals of greater complexity.

For example, one human generation lasts about twenty years while a virus generation may last only about twenty minutes. This means that one human generation is parallelled by about 500,000 virus generations.

Consequently, the human species would have to exist for 10 million years to be exposed to the same hazards of gene mutation and natural selection that viruses experience within a time space of only twenty years. But true man-like species are hardly 2 – 3 million years old.

To return to our main discussion, it can be shown that the distinction between sensory and reflex action is that the latter proceeds without memory. Thus reflex actions, like the heartbeat, the action of cell growth, the activity of breathing, of digestion, the action of swallowing food, etc., are automatic and are not memorized. The reason is that reflexes have no discriminative functions and therefore need no memory.

Sensory perceptions, on the other hand, have discriminatory functions and depend on memory. As a consequence, we find that a reflex action can short-circuit the brain, and, like instinct, is not involved in any thought process. On the other hand, even in unicellular life as well as in multicellular life (up to a certain stage before the possession of a brain) thought processes must take place. However one looks at the process of thinking or reasoning, it is basically nothing more than the coordination and association of differing sensations, firstly, by their quality and, secondly, in their intensity. Sense organs without discriminatory capacities would be an absurdity.

We see, then, that thinking, reasoning and intellectual activity all express the same capacity of living organisms: to compare and associate sense impressions of different kinds and of varying intensity. The primary objective of this combined action is the gathering of experience or learning in order to anticipate the vagaries of future situations. The ultimate aim is, of course, the maintenance of life and the preservation of the species.

Darwin has described an experiment with a pike which was put in an aquarium stocked with small fish, but was separated from them by a plate of glass. Driven by the urge to eat, the pike tried to catch the fish. But in so doing, he repeatedly ran his head against the dividing glass. Very often he was completely stunned by the impact, so that he eventually gave up. When the dividing glass was later removed, the pike, who could now have the fish, ignored them. However, when a different type of fish was put into the aquarium the pike did not hesitate; he caught and devoured them. (C. Darwin, 1871)

This example shows the presence of a complete thought process, where past experience in association with memories of pain served as a guide for future action, while the original cause of the whole chain of activities arose from the hunger instinct.

Other conspicuous examples of animal intelligence are certain ant species which use the plant juice-sucking aphids as milk cows. These ants regularly tap each aphid with their antennae, forcing it to exude drops of amber-coloured milk (honey-dew) from the horns of the abdomen. During the summer the aphids feed in the open on all kinds of plants and trees, while the ants herd them like cattle. When the aphids are moved to fresh pastures, they are not driven but are carried, each one bodily, in the ant-herds-men's jaws. Before winter comes, they are taken below ground, where they are fed on the stems of grasses or other roots which grow in or near the ants' nests. In this way the ants are provided with winter 'milk' just as man keeps his cows over the winter in a warm stable and feeds them. (A. Koestler, 1967.)

Carthy (quoted by Koestler) has cited evidence showing that some birds and mammals can recognize numbers. Beyond this they can match numbers and can remember them, and they will utilize that memory in future situations. For example, ravens, squirrels and parrots have been taught to take food from one particular bowl amongst a group of bowls distinguished by different numbers of black spots.

Thus it can be seen that, while the mental capacities of animals differ from those of man in degree, they are basically of the same potentiality. But in the absence of anything resembling human articulate speech, their usefulness has remained limited.

BIBLIOGRAPHY

Barnett, A., 1964. *The Human Species*, Collins, London.

Bailey, Geoff, 1983. *Hunter Gatherer Economy in Prehistory*, Cambr. Univ. Press, England.

Brace, C. and Montague, A., 1968. *Man's Evolution*, Collier, London.

Bray, W. and Trump D., 1970. *The Penguin Dictionary of Archaeology*, Penguin, England.

Bridewood, and Willey, 1962. *Courses Towards Urban Life*, Edinburgh University Press.

Bonin, G. von, 1963. *The Evolution of the Human Brain*, University of Chicago Press.

Caldwell, J.R., 1966. *New Roads to Yesterday*, Thames & Hudson, England.

Clark, D., 1968. In Symposium: 'Man The Hunter'.

Campbell, Bernhard, 1974. *Human Evolution*, Aldine Publishing Co., Chicago.

Campbell, Joseph, 1983. *The Way of The Animal Powers*, Harper & Row, San Francisco.

Childe, E.G., 1966. *Man Makes Himself*, Fontana Library, London.

Cippola, C.M., 1965. *The Economic History of World Populations*, Penguin.

Clark, G. and Piggott St., 1970. *Prehistoric Societies*, Penguin.

Clarke, R.J., see under Grusser, O.J., 1985.

Coon, C.S., 1967. *The History of Man*, Penguin.

Daniel, G., 1971. *The Early Civilizations*, Penguin.

Dart, R.A., 1957. *The Osteodontokeratic Culture of Australopithecus*, Transvaal Museum Mem. 10.

Dart, R.A., 1956. *Relationship of Brain Size and Brain Pattern to Human Status*, Southern African Journal of Medical Science 21: 23–45.

Darwin, C., 1859. *Origin of Species* I, John Murray, ed. London.

Darwin, C., 1866. *Origin of Species* IV Ed. John Murray, London.

Darwin, C., 1958. *Origin of Species*, Worlds Classics, Oxford University Press.

Darwin, C., 1871. *The Descent of Man*, John Murray, London.

Day, Michael H., 1977. *Guide to Fossil Man*, Cassel & Co., London.

Day, Michael H., 1973. *Human Evolution*, Society for the Study of Human Biology, Vol. 11, Taylor & Francis, London.

Day, M.H., Leakey, M.D. & Olson, T.R., 1980. On the Status of Australopithecus Africanus, Science pp. 1102–1103.

Encyclopaedia Brittanica, 1961 edition, England.

Encyclopaedia of Anthropology, 1976. Hunter D.E. and Whitten P., Harper & Row, N.Y.

Falk, Dean, 1980. *Hominid Brain Evolution: The Approach from Paleoneurology*, Yearbook of Ph. Anthr. 23:93–107, Alan R. Liss, N.Y.

Fiedel, S.T., 1987. *Prehistory of the Americas*, Cambridge University Press, England.

Flood, H., 1983. *Archaeology of the Dreamtime*, Collins, London.

Forde, Daryl C., 1968. *Habitat Economy and Society*, Methuen, London.

Franzen, J.L., see under Grusser, O.J., 1985.

Goodall, G., van Lawick, 1964. *Tool Using of free living Chimpanzees*, Nature, London. 201, 1264–6.

Gowlett, J., 1984. *Ascent to Civilization*, Collins, London.

Grusser, O.J. and Weiss L.R., 1985. *Hominid Evolution, Past, Present and Future* (Proceedings from Taung Diamond Jubilee), Alan R. Liss, Inc., New York.

Guilmet, G.M.: in MAN (1977, Vol. 12, No. 1) London.

Harris, M., 1968. *The Rise of Anthropology*, Routledge and Kegan Paul, London.

Harrison, A.J., *Man the Peculiar Animal*, Penguin.

Holloway, R.L., 1975. *The Role of Human Social Behavior in the Evolution of the Brain*. 43rs J. Arthur Lect., 1973. AMNH, N.Y.

Holloway, R.L., 1978. *The Relevance of Endocasts for Studying Primate Brain Evolution*, Plenum Publishers, N.Y., pp. 181–200.

Holloway, R.L., 1979. *Brain Size, Allometry, and Reorganization towards a Synthesis*. Academic Press, N.Y., pp. 59–88.

Holloway, R.L., 1984. 'The poor Brain of H. Neanderthalensis', in *Ancestors – The Hard Evidence*, Allan R. Liss, New York.

Howells, W.W., 1967. *Mankind in the Making*, Penguin.

Howells, W.W. and Trinkaus, 1980. In the *Scientific American*, U.S.A. (The Neanderthalrs: 94/105).

Huxley, J.S., 1957. *Evolution in Action*, Mentor Books, U.S.A.

Huxley, J.S., 1963. *Evolution: The Modern Synthesis*, Allen & Unwin, London.

Isaak, G.L., 1978. *The Archaelogical Evidence of the activities of Early African Hominids*, Duckworth, London.

Jairazbhoy, R.A., 1974. *Ancient Egyptians and Chinese in America*, London.

Jerison, H.J., 1970. *Gross Brain Indices and the Analysis of Fossil Endocasts*. The Primate Brain, 1255–44, N.Y.

Jerison, H.J., 1973. *Evolution of the Brain and Intelligence*. Academic Press, N.Y./London, 1–482.

Johanson, D.C. and Edey M.A. 1982. Lucy, *The Beginnings of Humankind*, Granada Publishing Ltd., England.

Koestler, A., 1967. *The Ghost in the Machine*, Hutchinson, London.

Kraus, G., 1973. *Homo Sapiens in Decline*, New Diffusionist Press, England.

Kraus, G., 1977. *Man in Decline*, St. Martin's Press, New York.

Kroeber, A.L., 1940. see under Daniel, G., 1971.

Leakey, M.D., 1971. *Olduvai Gorge Vol. 3. Excavations in Beds I and II*, Cambridge University Press.

Leakey, R.E. & Levin R., 1981. *People of the Lake*, Penguin.

Leakey, R.E., 1981. *The Making of Mankind*, Michael Joseph, London.

Liam de Paor, 1971. *Archaeology*, Pelican Original, England.

Lloyd, Seton, 1978. *Archaeology of Mesopotamia*, Thames & Hudson, London.

Lloyd, S. and Safar F., 1981. *Eridu*, Bagdad, (final official report).

Mc Henry, H.M., 1982. *The Pattern of Human Evolution*, American Review of Anthropology II, 151–173.

Mellaart, J., 1967. *The Earliest Settlements in Western Asia*, Cambridge University Press, England.

Parker, S.T. and Gibson, K.R., 1979. 'A Development Model for the Evolution of Language and Intelligence in Early

Hominids', The Behavioral & Brain Sciences 2. (367–381).

Passingham, R.E., 1975. 'The Brain and Intelligence'; Brain Behavioral Evolution, 2: 499–508.

Pilbeam, D., 1960. *The Evolution of Man*, Thames & Hudson, London.

Radinsky, L.B., 1979. *The Fossil Record of Primate Brain Evolution*. 49th James Arthur Lecture, American Museum of Natural History, N.Y.

Rench, B., 1959. *Evolution above the Species Level*, Methuen, London.

Rhodes, F.T.H., 1962. *The Evolution of Life*, Penguin.

Russell, Sir E. John, 1966. *The World of the Soil*, Penguin.

Shrire, Carmen, 1983. *Past and Present in Hunter Gatherer Studies*, Academic Press, N.Y./London (report on symposium at Bad Homburg, W. Germany – 13/16 June, 1983).

Simpson, G.G., *The Major Features of Evolution*, Columbia University Press, N.Y.

Soustelle, J., 1985 (1979). *The Olmecs*, Doubleday, N.Y.

Tobias, P.V., 1970. 'New Endocranial Volumes of Australopithecines', *Nature* 227: 199–200.

Tobias, P.V., 1971. *The Brain in Hominid Evolution*, Columbia University Press, N.Y./London.

Tobias, P.V., 1975. *Brain Evolution in the Hominidae*, (R.H. Tuttle, ed.) pp. 353–392, Mouton Publisher., The Hague, Holland.

Tobias, P.V., 1982. *The Antiquity of Man: Human Evolution, The Unfolding Genome*, Alan R. Liss, N.Y.

Tobias, P.V., 1983a, *Recent Advances in the Evolution of the Hominids: With Special Reference to Brain and Speech*, Pontifical Academy of Sciences – Scripta Varia, Vol. 50, pp. 85–140.

Tobias, P.V., 1983b, *Late Cainozoic Paleoclimates of the Southern Hemisphere*, Proceedings of the International Symposium of South African Society for Quarternary Res. A.A. Balkema/Rotterdam/Boston (Offprint).

Tobias, P.V., 1983c, *South African Hominids and the Evolution of Man*, Terra (pp. 11–15).

Tobias, P.V., 1985a, 'Punctuational and Phylelic Evolution in the Hominids' in Verba, E.S., ed., *Species and Speciation*, pp. 131–141, Transvall Museum, Pretoria.

Tobias, P.V., 1985b., 'Ten Climacteric Events in Hominid Evolution'. Reprint from South African Journal of Science, May, Vol. 81, No. 5.

Tobias, P.V., 1986. 'Delineation and Dating of some Major Phases In Hominidization since the Middle Miocene'. South African Journal of Medical Science, Vol. 82, pp. 92/94.

Tobias, P.V., 1987. 'The Brain of Homo Habilis: A New Level of Organization In Cerebral Evolution', Journal of Human Evolution.

Trigger et al, 1983. *Ancient Egypt – A Social History*, Cambridge University Press.

Turnbull, Colin M. 1966. *Wayward Servants*, Eyre & Spottiswood, London.

Turnbull, C.M., 1976. *Man in Africa*, Anchor Press/Doubleday, N.Y.

Turnbull, C.M., 1983. *The Mbuti Pygmies: Change and Adaptation*, Holt, Reinhard and Winston, New York.

White, Carmel, in Antiquity 1967. Vol. 41, 49/52.

Willey, G., see Bridewood and Willey, above.

Wolberg, D.L., 1970. 'Comment on Dart', in Current Anthropology II, 23-37.

Part II

A SCRUTINY OF CULTURAL THEORIES

FOREWORD

Much confusion is being caused in cultural theory by the continuing use of the inherently ambiguous term '*evolution*', this usage being outside its strictly biological context. Instead of considering *cultural* development as a transformation, change, or unfolding which is largely irregular and non-biological, both progressively and retrogressively, most social anthropologists imbue it with an aura of evolutionary biological progression. This despite the fact that cultural developments are not directly linked to biological factors. This is particularly noticeable in the lifestyle of culturally primitive hunter-gatherers[1] whose role I have defined in Part I, Chapter 7., as the First Category. They appear to have remained culturally stagnant over enormous periods.

1. HUNTER-GATHERER LIFE

S ome general facts about hunter-gatherers, particularly their
division into three different cultural categories owing to
lesser or greater complexity or sophistication in their lifestyle,
has already been dealt with in preceding Part I (Chapter 7).
There the main concern was with the material and technological
aspect of hunter-gatherer life; here the focus will be more on it
social and ideological content.

R. Leakey (1981) pointed out that Nineteenth-century
anthropologists viewed hunter-gatherers as fossilized societies;
primitive savages who had somehow slipped unnoticed and
unnoticing into the modern world. Leakey thinks that this view
is nonsensical. The hunter-gatherers were as modern in biological terms as the explorers who discovered them. They just
happened to sustain themselves by an ancient method.
Anthropologist Marshall Sahlins (as quoted by Leakey) has
argued that Western anthropologists must not impose Western,
that is, materialistic ethics on their subjects. Sahlins refers to the
different goals of the various societies: the pursuit of wealth,
property and prestige in the one, and something totally different
in the other. He goes so far as to suggest that the hunting and
gathering way of life is the original affluent society in which all
the peoples' wants are easily satisfied. As it happens, the
hunting and gathering economy is not an incessant search for
food, as many anthropologists have supposed, but a system that
allows a great deal more leisure than is possible in either agricultural or industrial society.

Some details about culturally primitive food-gathering
groups deserve recall in this context. Schebesta (1929:53) has
described the 'negritos' of Malaya as: 'primitive relics, almost,
of a prehistoric age, and, "savages" by name only. Their affection towards each other was strong and their little camp had an
air of contentment. Their fundamental unit is a small group of

relatives. There is no chiefly class, no tribal unity'. Another group, the Kubu of Sumatra were observed by Forbes (1885:232) to be as peaceful and having no social classes. He says that until a few years ago they wore no clothes, and concludes that: 'one cannot help feeling that they are harmless, overgrown, children of the woods'. Others like the Punan of Borneo were culturally speaking, among the most primitive people in the world. Hose and McDougall (1912:180/185), described them as having no social classes, no houses, and their property was held communally. Harmony and mutual help were the rule within their family circle, as well as throughout their larger groupings; the men generally treated their wives and children with kindness and the women performed their duties cheerfully and faithfully. Schebesta spoke of the Semang of Malaya (1929:279) as having no tribal organization; while Forde observed that they were unable to fashion even simple pebble tools (1968:70).

Many social anthropologists hold the view that the allegedly peaceful and rather idyllic life-style of culturally primitive food-gatherers (past and present) is more myth than reality and that they have been just as aggressive and superstitious as their materially more advanced agricultural and pastoral neighbours. In this respect the remarks of Mayer Fortes at a Symposium (1973:431) are typical: 'No human group has yet been discovered which is devoid of some form of extra social organization, leadership, ritual practices, or aggressive tendencies'. In support he referred to the field researches of Radcliffe-Brown, among the Andmanese; the Seligmans among the Veddahs of Ceylon; and the field-researches of Father Wilhelm Schmidt of the Vienna School from 1906 onwards. A study of the Mbuti and similar foodgathering groups, which I shall cite in due course, will serve as a rebuttal of these views.

However, in certain respects Fortes' observations are valid for those surviving food-gatherers and hunters listed in category three and even two (see Chapter 7) who have been greatly affected by their contacts with semi-civilized and civilized populations. The recent history of the Khoi-San (so-called Bushmen) of South Africa, commented upon by Dorman (1925:43) is a

111

case in point. 'Although the Bushmen had already been driven from their original homeland in the Cape by advancing Bantu-speaking Negroes, they could still be described on the whole as happy, lively people, full of merriment ... though when opposed or thwarted they could become savage, cruel and vindictive .... When the Dutch arrived at the Cape at 1650, they slaughtered the game on which the Bushmen lived and took away their land. In self-defence the latter took to looting the Dutchmen's herds, and in retaliation were shot like wild beasts, while the women and children were carried into slavery (1925:205/206)'. Despite these ordeals, the Kung (the section of Bushmen who occupy part of the Kalahari desert), have preserved some of their original ethics.'

Thus, Lee (cited by R. Leakey, 1981): 'Sharing of resources deeply pervades the behaviour and values of Kung foragers within the family and between families, and it is extended to the boundaries of the social universe. This ethic is not confined to the Kung; it is a feature of hunter-gatherers in general. In the same vein as the sharing ethic, comes a surprising degree of egalitarianism. The Kung have no chiefs and no leaders ... disputes are readily defused through communal bantering. No one gives orders or takes them'.

Further afield in Asia the fate of some food-gathering tribes of India was reported by Buchanan (1867). He travelled through Mysore, Canara, and Malabar, and observed that: 'In nearly all cases they have been subjected to slavery at the hands of their neighbours, and in their service have learned the rudiments of agriculture and other arts'.

These and countless other instances show that c. 6000 years of contact with semi-civilized and civilized populations has inevitably tainted and corrupted the cultures of primitive food-gatherers and saddled them with many of the customs and social attributes of sedentary tribal societies.[1] It is surprising that many of these culturally primitive groups have not become even more influenced in their basic nature and life-style by such extensive cohabitation. Thus we find some surviving examples (among them most prominent the Mbuti who have remained relatively free from such social complexities.[2]

The significance of the Twa-Mbuti (so-called pygmies) of the Congo as they were found by Colin Turnbull in the 1950s rests not so much on the material aspect of their culture, but on its ideological content. In revealing their basic mentality with its no-nonsense attitude to foreign belief-systems and social attitudes, Turnbull has made a major contribution to the ethnological sciences, which given due recognition, could greatly affect current ideas prevalent in social anthropology. He discovered that the Twa-Mbuti still bore (or almost bore) no tribalistic ideology or philosophy, although they had been in reported contact with the outside world for thousands of years.[3]

Thus, writes Turnbull (in the *Scientific American*, 1963: Jan.): 'After centuries of contact with the "more advanced" cultures of the villages and inspite of all appearances, their acculturation to any other mode of life remains almost nil'. And again in *African Pygmies* (1986), he says: 'The pyramidal edifice of family, lineage and clan does not exist in any form. There is no intermediate grouping between family and band, and none between band and total population, ... The solidarity of the band is the prime factor in ensuring group survival, in which kinship once again plays a minimal role'. Also according to Turnbull (1966), and I quote at length,

> The overall picture of the present Mbuti culture is one of a society where the lack of formal structure is so evident that one wonders why there is no complete disintegration. There are not only no chiefs or councils of elders, but no ritual specialists, and no lineage system, and no body of beliefs in super-natural sanction. The only effective political unit is the band, which can be defined as a unit of Mbuti sharing and recognising a common hunting territory. Membership of the band is fluid.
>
> *Kinship*: Neither men nor women are able to name their grandparents (nor even to name any brother or sister of their grandparents), unless they have a vivid personal recollection of them. The only occasion of any significance to such detail would be marriage.
>
> *Initiation and Marriage*: Though manhood is every bit as important to the Mbuti as to the villagers, there is no formal Mbuti initiation ritual.[4] And although marriage is considered just as sacred, it takes place in the forest in an apparently utterly casual manner, without any ceremony or ritual joining the boy and the girl or their families ....
>
> *Death* is accepted as a natural event and does not lead to any accu-

sation of witch-craft or sorcery, except in a Bantu village context. Burial is performed simply and quickly and excessive display of grief is frowned upon. The forest procedure (of natural death) would simply be to bury the body, then abandon the camp and build a new one, never again mentioning the dead person.

As to the Mbuti's Belief-System, Turnbull observed:

> *Magic*: The Mbuti have no magic with which to counter magic, and no witchcraft to counter witchcraft or sorcery (1966:54). As to witchcraft seen as a malevolent sorcery; they cannot believe that a 'bundle of sticks' is going to afford much help (1966:59).
> *Religious afterlife*: The Mbuti say: 'that to try and go into the future is to walk blindly', and their response to their Bantu masters and missionaries, or any who claim knowledge of afterlife, is: 'How do you know, have you died and been there before?'
> *The Super-natural*: Among the Mbuti there is a belief in a power greater than themselves, which is not of the natural order or of the world as they see it around them. They explain these unknown forces with a rather confused terminology;[5] The Epelu Mbuti use five different terms and these are drawn from Lese, Bira, and Ndaka, which are all settled villages of their Bantu masters among whom they live.
> *Godhead*: The Mbuti strenuously refuse to admit that there is any sense in trying to describe what we call here 'godhead'. They will say: 'Unless you have seen it there is no sense in accepting it'.

In judging the discoveries of Turnbull, one must note the rare coincidence of his finding the Mbuti when they were still in a socially and, ideationally, fairly uncontaminated state, just at the eleventh hour, before their almost inevitable demise as a cultural prototype.[6] It is difficult to recall any similar discovery taking place so close to the end of an era ever to recur in human history, and such a coincidence is very unlikely to occur again.

Most social anthropologists consider the kinship syndrome an axiomatic and universally applicable feature in the evolution of societies. Its virtual non-existence among the Mbuti and some other culturally 'low-level' hunter-gatherers seems to negate this assumption. While the Mbuti show an almost total absence of super-natural ideas, it is a fact that they acquired some confused notions about a superior power. However, considering their rejection of the notions of a 'godhead' and of a 'religious there-after', it is likely that such precepts were assimilated during the

Mbuti's long exposure to culturally more complex societies. Such a partial relapse can hardly be attributed to the Mbuti's having receded from a former socially and ideationally more complex stage. On the contrary, given the commonsense attitude generally exhibited by the Mbuties we can assume that before they became saddled with any such ideatic burdens they could only have been ideationally less complex than their modern descendants.

In Asia thousands of miles apart from the Twa-Mbuti of the Congo we have examples of hunter-gatherers resembling them in some aspects of their mentality, though to a lesser degree in their total rejection of paranormal ideas and the absence of social conventions. Although living in similar conditions to the Mbuti these people have been more subject to foreign influences. Among other less typical examples are the African Khoi-San (so-called Bushmen) of the Kalahari desert in South Africa.

From the example of the Mbuti we can presume that the mentality of pre-historic hunter-gatherers as a whole, in respect of social customs and their world of ideas, could only have been less complex ideationally than that of their presently surviving culturally ultra-'primitive' successors (i.e., those listed in our Category One). Although the available evidence may serve as a general indicator of the ideological status of hunter gatherers the world over during the preceding hundreds of thousands of years, before food-producing societies became prominent there is no direct evidence to support this claim.

In material culture, similar analogies are possible, between modern and prehistoric hunter-gatherers. Yet as in the above, they are largely based on circumstantial evidence. On the other hand, many anthropologists assert that this type of analogy is not feasible. Commenting on a previous draft of this paper, social anthropologist Edmund Leach writes (personal communication): 'A substantial portion of the authors you mention believed that ethnographic evidence could be used to reconstruct the history of the distant past. You yourself seem to believe this even though you are sceptical concerning most efforts of this kind. I myself would agree with those other anthropologists (with whom most serious historians would also agree) who say that it is impossible to reconstruct history on the basis of circumstantial evidence'.

Similar views have been expressed by Gowlett (1984). He writes: 'Any direct analogy between modern hunter-gatherers and societies represented in the archaeological evidence would be unwise .... Analogy is especially suspect when the practice of one modern people is invoked to explain apparently similar behaviour in the past, for usually there are many other possibilities'.

Inspite of these objections I maintain that some degree of comparison between the material cultures of prehistoric and modern hunter-gatherers is possible. In this respect, the cultural propensities of Homo habilis, as summarised by Tobias (1983) serve as a useful starting point. Much of what I have to say has already been referred to in Part I.

To begin with, for a hominid emerging between 2.3 and 1.75 million years ago, the stone-tool capacities of Homo habilis are most impressive. The respective cultural assembly designated Oldowan (M.D. Leakey, 1971), includes a predominance of tools known as choppers, while other forms recognised are proto-bifaces, polyhedrons, discoids, spheroids and subspheroids, heavy-duty and light-duty scrapers, burins and sundry other tools. Of the choppers, five types have been described: side, end, two-edged, pointed and chisel-edged.

Considering this variegated arsenal c. 2 million years old of stone tools, it is interesting to note that some modern hunter-gatherers, like the Semang and the Ik, show no stone tool-making capacities at all, and until recent history relied on unworked natural stone debris to do the job, while the Mbuti (at least in living memory), neither made stone tools, nor used natural stone debris for tools. Still more remarkable is the observation elaborated in Part I that only a minority of prehistoric hunter-gatherers, throughout the millions of years preceding agriculture, were active stone tool-makers, while the vast majority used stones casually for tools without taking the trouble to fashion them into shape, just as contemporary Semang and Ik did until recently. If we therefore judge cultural progress in terms of stone tool technology alone, we must put Homo habilis of 2 million years ago on a higher cultural level than the vast bulk of prehistoric hunter-gatherers who followed them, including some recent survivors.[7]

As to the other cultural capabilities of Homo habilis (apart from stone tools), Tobias lists the following: The construction of some form of shelters, indicating stone-walling, the aimed throwing of missiles, the butchery of large animal carcasses with stone tools, the transport of meat and other foods to a home base, delayed consumption, the sharing of food and its distribution to members of the group, etc. Tobias further indicates that the evidence of such propensities, both observed and inferred, has been delineated among others by such authors as M.D. Leakey (1971), Isaak (1978) and Parker and Gibson (1979), though admittedly not without being challenged. Most outspoken among such critics is Edmund Leach, who bluntly observed (personal communication), that 'We know nothing whatsoever about the "culture complex of Homo habilis". Why pretend otherwise?'

I believe that Leach's judgement is rather offhand, since we find most of the activities outlined above (with the exception of Homo habilis' elaborate stone-tool technology and the construction of stone-walling), incorporated in the material cultures of many modern hunter-gatherer peoples, with the addition of intrusive cultural elements derived over the millennia from culturally more complex neighbours.

Let us instance the aimed throwing of missiles together with the butchering of large animal carcasses. During the recovery of Homo habilis' fossils at Olduvai, a large amount of animal bones were also found. Some of the larger bones were found broken into many pieces, in a way that would not have been possible by the action of predatory animals; meaning, that the bones must have been fractured by human hands (possibly to extract the marrow). Besides, some of the bones showed tell-tale marks, indicating the use of sharp stone-tools for butchering purposes. To carry out these operations and deal with such remains, the animals had, of course, to be killed first. For this purpose, spears for use as missiles and lances for thrusting were the logical, and obviously the only suitable implements available in these early times. There is hardly any alternative to spears and lances, not only to hunt game but to defend against large predators such as lions and panthers. Without their aid, early man (i.e., Homo habilis) would have been utterly defenceless, and could not have survived. As to carrying food, its storage, distribution and sharing, these are biological propensities which can be assumed to have been acquired by hominids, when an inordinately long period of child care required such attributes. They were essential for survival and therefore favoured by natural selection. One could probably speculate, and add to this arsenal some requisites for carrying loads – the use of digging sticks, and even the use of nets and traps to catch animals; though unfortunately such perishable articles leave no trace in the archaeological record.

Having adopted these essentials, few cultural attributes of equal importance remain to differentiate the basic cultural equipment of Homo habilis from that of modern, culturally primitive hunter-gatherers. And if not quite equalling them, they certainly seem to deviate little from that basic cultural equipment possessed by later, prehistoric, culturally under-developed, hunter-gatherers, who had additionally adopted the use of fire, and the bow and arrow. Here it must be remembered that the use of fire goes back 1½ million years or more. The use of the bow and arrow may also go further back than has hitherto been assumed. Their earliest use has been deduced from the find of 40,000 year old microliths in Africa which supposedly served as arrow-points (Gowlett, 1984). However, the fact that the Mbuti prefer the use of fire-hardened wood points to stone tipped arrows, suggests the possibility that the general use of bow and arrow may go back still earlier.

In consideration of the above and the inferences drawn one is led to the conclusion that the material culture of modern, culturally primitive hunter-gatherers resembles in its most important fundamentals that of their prehistoric forbears, just as is suggested for the social and ideological aspect of their life.

2. CULTURAL 'EVOLUTIONISM'

To repeat, much ambiguity has resulted by the non-separation of the biological aspect of evolution from the cultural one. The root cause dates back to Herbert Spencer who introduced the term evolution to describe the transmutation in organic life in the aftermath of Lamarck and Darwin, applying it to cultural phenomena as well. Spencer and his disciples placed man on the top of the evolutionary ladder, with cultural evolution being considered a continuation of human biological evolution. In this context, cultural evolution attained a biological status by becoming linked with Lamarckian inheritance. I shall elaborate on the origin and continuity of this idea in due course, but note meanwhile that with the advent of genetics and the consequent downfall of Lamarckism the idea of cultural evolution also became outdated, since it could not now be upheld on the basis of the theory of genetic inheritance which followed.

In the strict sense, therefore, the term 'cultural evolution' has become outmoded, and should be substituted by the phrase 'cultural development', growth or change, while at the same time stressing its separateness from biology. A close look at cultural aptitudes throughout the ages shows (as detailed in Part I) three periods of differing cultural developments. Two of these relate to culturally developing hominids, and the third to culturally under-developed ones. The first period denoted here as pre-Homo sapiens, stretches over several million years and includes the lithic cultures of Australopithecus, Homo habilis and Homo erectus. *During this period, up to c. 300,000 B.P. (the advent of Homo sapiens), average brain sizes increased from c. 350 cc, to c. 1200 and 1350 cc. Yet in spite of this c. 1000 cc increase in brain volume, the accompanying cultural developments, even of the culturally more advanced hominids, were no more than modest.*

The second developmental period extends over the entire Homo sapiens sequence of c. 300,000 years, during which average brain volume remained fairly constant at c. 1350 cc. As to cultural aptitudes, during the first half (c. 150,000 years) of this period, Homo sapiens did not exceed (as far as it is known) the cultural level of their predecessor, Homo erectus. Then, from c. 150,000 B.P. to c. 10,000 B.P., in its latter stages, groups of Neanderthalers and later Cromagnon, showed some remarkable cultural achievements. Yet comparatively seen, even these lagged far behind those of the following Neolithic sequence which marks the advent of domestication, lagging even more behind those of civilization. And yet these latter spectacular cultural achievements were not paralleled by increased brain sizes which had remained stagnant on a world level of around 1350 cc for c. 300,000 years. *Neither is there any biological evidence* (see Part I, Chapter 6), *that the intellectual qualities of the human brain, as seen apart from its purely cubic content or weight, had increased in any noticeable degree during Homo sapiens' late cultural upsurge.*

The third developmental period embraces the culturally under-developed section of humanity (a subject dealt with at length in Part I, Chapter 7). Although the respective hominids equalled their culturally developing contemporaries biologically throughout all stages of their evolution from Australopithecus to Homo sapiens, they stagnated culturally at a level prevalent during the Stone-Age. Some culturally ultra-primitive modern hunter-gatherers can still bear witness to this fact.

The only plausible conclusion to be drawn from the above account is that brain development had little bearing on cultural events. Vice versa, nor is there any indication, specifically during the Homo sapiens sequence, that cultural developments had any biological association.

The Origins of the belief in Cultural Evolutionism can be traced back to events which followed Columbus' discovery of America. Returning explorers, missionaries and adventurers who swarmed the world brought back a flood of accounts relating to newly discovered lands and their populations. There followed more systematic explorations, when governments and learned societies sent out geographers, naturalists and ethnologists. The latter included Alexander von Humboldt and Charles Darwin, and in more recent times the Seligmans, Radcliffe-Brown and Malinowski, also W.H.R. Rivers, A.C. Haddon, and A.M. Hocart, to mention just a few; while armchair ethnologists such as James Frazer catalogued and analysed the collected material. One astonishing discovery thereby noted was that many of the newly observed strange customs, institutions, and beliefs had identical counterparts in widely dispersed areas of the world, a fact amply documented by Frazer in *The Golden Bough*, among others.

How did these ethnological discoveries become linked with concepts of evolution? It is suggested that the original impetus emanated from Darwin's work *The Origin of Species*, which was the result of the observations he made during his voyage aboard the *Beagle* in his capacity as naturalist. *The Origin of Species* became subsequently the catalyst for biological evolutionary ideas of the last century. Darwin supplied the framework whereby all species of organic life could be related to a common ancestry. Within this biological universe, the transmutation of living-forms was perpetrated by natural selection. Darwin had a predecessor in Lamarck, who attributed such changes (or transmutations) to a mode of inheritance based on the transmission of characteristics acquired during life-time and affected by the greater or lesser use of organs and the direct influence on the organism of external conditions.

In fairness to Lamarck, whose theory of heredity has incidentally largely been discarded, Darwin himself adopted part of Lamarck's inheritance theory, and even attempted to rationalize it in his theory of 'pangenesis'. Despite such diversions Darwin's biological evolutionary views remained principally based on natural selection with minor concessions to Lamarckian heredity. In contrast, Lamarck's theory omitted all notions of natural selection, since at his time they were scarcely known.[1]

Also Darwin showed only passing interest in ethnological science, his main efforts being devoted to the universal process of organic life in which Homo sapiens played only a marginal role.[2] Lamarck and his followers on the other hand devoted themselves more to Homo sapiens and his cultural life. Thus

Adolf Bastian, an ardent follower of Lamarck (a German scholar born in 1826 when Darwin was 17 years old), argued that by a general law, the psychic unity of man everywhere produced similar ideas .... This led in turn to the belief in the independent evolution of culture. Glyn Daniel (1964:91) described Bastian's theory as a form of 'super-organic, or cultural, or social evolution'.

Herbert Spencer's (a contemporary of Darwin) ideas on the subject were similar to Bastian's though more specific. Freeman (1974:216), has pointed out that 'by 1873 Spencer had systematically extended his fervently held Lamarckian beliefs to human social evolution. Spencer had advanced the theory that the mental and social evolution of the species Homo sapiens was primarily caused by the inheritance of acquired characteristics producing gradual and inevitable modifications of human nature and human institutions'.

Spencer was not alone in holding Lamarckian views; even Darwin subscribed to them to a degree, and both were later joined by such authorities as E.B. Tylor, Lewis Morgan, James Frazer, and others. They developed the theory of 'Unilinear Cultural Evolution' as the best possible explanation available at the time for the presence of identical cultural traits paralleled in different parts of the world.[3]

Unilinealism in culture arose from the idea that the cultural evolution of Homo sapiens was a continuation of his biological evolution. In unilinear cultural evolution it is assumed that cultural patterns in different parts of the world are genetically unrelated and yet pass through parallel sequences. E.B. Tylor, for example, proposed an evolutionary cultural line of human progress uniformly applicable throughout the world passing through the stages of Savagery and Barbarism to Civilization (*Anthropology*, 1881); while Lewis Morgan spoke of an inevitable cultural evolution passing through seven different stages – leading separately in Egypt, China, and Middle America, to the civilizations of literate cities (Daniel, 1964:68).

At a later stage Freud, Jung, and other psychologists thought in similar cultural patterns. According to Freud (following Frazer): in an evolutionary sequence magic is succeeded by religion in which man surrenders part of his powers to supernatural beings, and this in turn is succeeded by science. Freud's biographer and pupil Ernst Jones relates (1961:296) that like Spencer, Freud was an ardent Lamarckist: 'Freud early cherished the Lamarckian belief to which he had adhered throughout his life'. And in a letter to Ferenczi (1961:442), Freud remarked: 'Our intention is to place Lamarckism entirely on our basis and show that "need" which created and transformed organs is nothing other than the power of unconscious ideas over the body ... in short, the "omnipotence of thought"'. Another Freud biographer, Wolheim (1971:219) remarked that Freud himself did not articulate any coherent social theory. Yet contemporary ethnologists (among them Lévi-Strauss) have eagerly formulated ethnological theories related to Freudian and Jungian tenets,[4] despite the latter's Lamarckian tendencies which have long since been discarded in the light of genetic science. Thus it can no longer be maintained that there is a physiological mechanism in the human make up based on the genes which explains how Lamarckian inheritance can be produced.[5]

The prevailing view held by most modern biologists about Lamarckian inheritance has been competently summarised by Julian Huxley (1957:35):

> With the knowledge which has been amassed since Darwin's time it is no longer possible to believe that evolution is brought about through so-called inheritance of acquired characters – the direct effect of use or disuse of organs, or of changes in the environment, or by the conscious will of organisms, or through the operation of some mysterious vital force, or by any other inherent tendency. What this means in the terms of biology is that all the theories lumped together under the heads of orthogenesis and Lamarckism are invalidated .... They are ruled out: they are no longer consistent with the facts. Indeed, in the light of modern discoveries they no longer deserve to be called a scientific theory but more as speculation or even superstition disguised in modern dress.[6]

Inspite of the eclipse of Lamarckism, and later the rejection of unilinear cultural evolution (now dismissed as obsolete by a majority of contemporary anthropologists), it can be shown that the tenets of both continue to hound contemporary ethnological and social anthropological thought under such labels as multi-linear cultural evolutionism, functionalism and structuralism. If closely analysed, almost all these theories have basically remained either directly or indirectly Lamarck orientated, as are most other theories linked to the concept of cultural evolution. Why? Since they cannot be explained in terms of natural selection and genetic inheritance, they must in the last resort depend on Lamarckian factors to justify their existence.

On the other hand, the dependency of biological evolutionary concepts on natural selection as the final arbiter is now firmly established in modern biological evolutionary theory and finds expression in Julian Huxley's dictum (1957:75) that: '*No evolutionary trend can be maintained except by natural selection*,[7] *and natural selection can only work on what is biologically useful to its possessors*'.

The process of biological evolution has been described by Darwin as 'descent by modification'. Darwin himself used the word 'evolution', a term actually originated by Spencer, only in his later years.[8] One can now expand on this in the light of post-Darwinian genetic science (i.e. Neo-Darwinism), and propose that biological evolution is the continuous diversification of living forms perpetrated by genetic inheritance under the influence of natural selection. It involves no directional or necessarily progressive principle.

Consequently, the term 'evolution' when applied to cultural or social processes is misplaced, and can only be rationally used in a biological sequence, based on genetics and natural selection. It is significant that one of the leading anthropologists of our day, Lévi-Strauss (1968:3) admitted the derivation of this idea by saying: 'The evolutionist interpretation in anthropology clearly derives from evolutionism in biology'. In the face of this significant admission most contemporary social anthropologists have remained blinkered to this truth.

3. MULTILINEAR CULTURAL EVOLUTION

To reiterate, nowadays practically all social anthropologists and ethnologists reject the Lamarckian-linked theory of unilinear cultural evolution as obsolete. This includes leading multilinealists such as A.L. Kroeber (who had earlier revoked it), as well as J.R. Caldwell, J.H. Steward, and Glyn Daniel. But while they have abandoned unilinealism in favour of multilinealism, it can be shown that while rejecting the former theory in its abstract, they still follow its basic tenets in practice.

Glyn Daniel, in *The First Civilizations* (1971) deals competently with the archaeological background preceding the emergence of the early civilizations. But in his conclusions relating to the actual origin of these civilizations he vacillates. In a previous work *The Idea of Prehistory* (1964:91), he defined unilinear cultural evolution (which he rejects) as '*a form of super-organic or cultural or social evolution*'. Seven years later in *The First Civilizations*, he described multilinear evolution in practically the same terms as '*a supra-organic, a cultural evolution in man's development*'; calling it: 'the basic principle of the culture-process which leads to civilization' (1971:176–177). A closer examination reveals that both definitions are identical, and since in the same paragraph, he attributes a like trend of thought to other multilinealist colleagues such as Kroeber and Caldwell, we can see that all these cultural theorists are unable to clearly distinguish between what is unilinear and what is multilinear in cultural evolution. That both are in fact identical is confirmed by Leslie White, the doyen of cultural evolutionism. He wrote (1959:30/31): 'Evolutionist interpretations of culture will be both unilinear and multilinear. One type of interpretation is as valid as the other, each implies the other'.

Furthermore, according to dictionary definition[1] both terms '*super organic*' and '*supra-organic*' are conceptions which reach outside, or beyond, the realms of any earthly, organic, or biological existence. To somehow mitigate this metaphysical aspect, multilinear cultural evolutionism as explained by Daniel, holds that unialism (the discarded thesis) is universally applicable, while multilinealism (its acceptable replacement) has a restricted, selective application.[2] In effect, the above demonstrates, that both, unilinear and multilinear cultural evolution, are subject to the same super-organic, metaphysical guiding principles, placing them firmly outside any biological evolutionary conception.

This obviously determinist interpretation of multilinealism is endorsed by its originators. Kroeber (1940) maintained that: 'We must consider that civilization *is an inevitable response to laws governing the growth of culture and controlling the man-culture relationship*'; and Caldwell: 'Perhaps there is only one finite number of social and historical processes *behind the events of history*'; while Daniel comments (1971:176): 'I think Caldwell and Kroeber are right' .... We should now think in terms of multilineal evolution, *leading inevitably*, as Kroeber said, for some ... societies with geographical and ecological and cultural possibilities to synoecism, one of the finite number of social and historical *processes behind the events of history*. Daniel concludes: 'I believe that an interpretation of the origins of civilization in terms of multilineal evolution is in accordance with the archaeological facts as known to us'.[3]

The above emphasised phrases express the true nature of multilinear thinking, whereby multilinealist cultural evolution is revealed as a concept guided throughout by determinist super-organic forces, which, in substance places it in the sphere of the paranormal.

It is also notable that none of the preceding expositions on multilinear cultural evolution mention any biological linkage in terms of modern genetics, a trend apparent in the work of J.H. Steward, a leading theorist on the subject. While discussing at length cultural evolution vis-a-vis biological evolution, he concludes (1953:11/14), that the former (i.e. cultural evolution) has no biological association. This is in accord with Daniel's previously mentioned definition of a super, or supra-organic process. Steward further says that: 'The mythology of evolution contains two vitally important assumptions. First, it postulates that genuine parallels of form and function develop in historically independent sequences or cultural traditions. Second, it explains these parallels by the *independent operation of identical causality'*.

Again, the emphasised words point to a process linked to Lamarckism, based on the fact that culture is created by human beings and they could only produce parallel cultural traits independently in response to identical conditions of life (i.e., identical causality in a Lamarckian sense); this in turn depends on hereditary predispositions moulded by 'identical causality'. In other words, man's parallel cultural expressions are said to be shaped by acquired characteristics which are inheritable, this being an example of the equal working of the human mind in response to like circumstances. In short, we have here an endorsement of Bastian's principle of the 'psychic unity' attributable to all mankind. In its essence it implies a biological process based on Lamarckian inheritance.

Steward elaborates this Lamarckian reasoning as follows:

> Cultural evolution, then, may be defined broadly as a quest for cultural regularities or laws; but there are three distinctive ways in which evolutionary data may be handled. First, unilinear evolution, the classical nineteenth century formulation, dealt with particular cultures, placing them in stages of universal sequence. Second, universal evolution – a rather arbitrary label to designate the modern revamping of unilinear evolution – is concerned with culture rather than with cultures. Third, *multilinear evolution*, a somewhat less ambitious approach than the other two, *is like unilinear evolution* (my emphasis) in dealing with developmental sequences, but it is distinctive in searching for parallels of limited occurrence instead of universals.

Thus multilinear evolution is presented here as a variation of unilinear evolution, a view endorsed by Lesley White (see above).

The passage from Steward cited above (1953:14) is followed by many pages of involuted reasoning attempting to substantiate his view, but in effect carrying very little conviction.[4]

127

In the light of such attempts the conception of multilinear cultural evolution presents a remarkable aberration in ethnological thought. It can perhaps by explained by its proponents conjuring a smoke screen against cultural diffusionist explanations, and in the process taking recourse to irrational arguments and verbally elusive pseudo-scientific jargon.

This may appear a rather harsh judgement, although it is far less out-spoken than the comments of the great scholar Bertauld Laufer. In a review of Lowie's 'Culture and Ethnology' (*American Anthropology* 1918, 20:87/8). Laufer wrote: 'The theory of cultural evolution, to my mind, is the most inane, sterile and pernicious theory ever conceived in the history of science, (a cheap toy for the amusement of big children) .... Culture cannot be forced into a straight-jacket of any theory whatever it may be, nor can it be reduced to chemical or mathematical formulae. All that the practical investigator can hope for, at least for the present, is to study each cultural phenomenon as exactly as possible in its geographical distribution, its historical development and its relation or association with kindred ideas'.

4. THE STRUCTURALIST APPROACH

Structuralism is basically an attempt by ethnological theorists, explicitly differing with diffusionist and evolutionist interpretations of social and cultural phenomena, to replace or supplement them by structuralist solutions. They assert that common social phenomena like beliefs, institutions, customs, rituals, myths, totems and taboos, can be explained by the working of underlying 'deep' or 'hidden' structures such as collective dreams and unconscious wishes.[1] French anthropologist Lévi-Strauss (1968:3) has maintained that the structuralist approach to culture has no cultural evolutionist associations. An analysis of its basic concepts as given suggests otherwise.

While structural analysis (originally used in linguistics), presents a quite novel approach to cultural theory, it gained notoriety when applied and expanded upon by Lévi-Strauss, who is perhaps better described as a structuralist philosopher. Some of his expressions as exemplified by Edmund Leach are products of ethnological fantasies straying into poetry.

Leach, a prominent English theorist who is both an admirer and critic of Lévi-Strauss, has praised the truly poetic range of associations which Lévi-Strauss brings to bear in the course of his analyses (1970:118), but at the same time he subjected Lévi-Strauss to harsh criticism.[2]

Lévi-Strauss adopts a more realistic approach when dealing with 'parallel art forms' under the heading 'The Split Representations in the art of Asia and America' he writes (1968:246/248):

> It is impossible not to be struck by the analogies presented by the Northwest Coast and ancient Chinese art. These analogies derive not so much from the external aspect of the objects as from the fundamental principles which an analysis of both arts yields.
> ... Once these similarities have been noted, it is curious to observe that, for entirely different reasons, ancient Chinese and Northwest Coast art have been independently compared with Maori art in New Zealand ....
> Do we rest, then, on the horns of a dilemma which condemns us to deny history or to remain blind to similarities so often confirmed?
> ... We reserve, therefore, the right to compare American Indian art with that of China or New Zealand, even if it has been proved a thousand times over that the Maori could not have brought their weapons and ornaments to the Pacific Coast. Cultural contact doubtless constitutes the one hypothesis which most easily accounts for complex similarities that chance cannot explain. But if historians maintain that contact is impossible, this does not prove that the similarities are illusory, but only that one must look elsewhere for the explanation. The fruitfulness of the diffusionist approach derives precisely from its systematic exploration of the possibilities of history. If history, when it is called upon unremittingly (and it must be called upon first), cannot yield an answer, *then let us appeal to psychology, or the structural analysis of forms*; let us ask ourselves if internal connections, whether of a psychological or logical nature, will allow us to understand parallel recurrences whose frequency and cohesion cannot possibly be the result of chance'. (my emphasis)

This recourse to psychology as a final arbiter to problems which Lévi-Strauss feels cannot be resolved by diffusion, re-occurs in most of the other Lévi-Straussian ethnological theories, whether they deal with kinship systems, myths, religion, or pure semantics.

Discussing Lévi-Strauss's pre-occupation with kinship-systems, Leach observes (1970:95): 'Although there are thousands of different human languages, all kin term systems belong to one or other of about half a dozen "types"; how should we explain this? Lévi-Strauss does not follow Lewis Morgan at all closely but he assumes, as we might expect, that any particular system of kin terms is a syntagem of the 'system' of all possible systems, which is in turn a precipitate of *a universal human psychology*'. (my italics)

Such reliance on psychology is a return to Bastian's (Lamarck based), 'Psychic Unity of All Mankind', where it forms the basis of unilinear cultural evolutionism, a principle continued by Frazer, Freud, Jung and others and now endorsed by Lévi-Strauss. The fact that the bulk of mankind, the primitive food-gatherers of all ages, are excluded from this assumedly universal state of affairs, renders it illusionary. A few brief examples can substantiate this. Morris (1976:543) found many Hill Pandaram (India-based primitive food-gatherers) could not remember the names even of their grandparents, a condition which Turnbull had also noted among the Mbuti pygmies of the Congo. Leach (1970:105), has pointed out that the majority of what are by some ethnologists usually considered to be surviving 'ultra primitives' (e.g., Congo Twa and Kalahari Khoi-San)[3] do not have kinship systems of unilinear descent (considered to be the simplest form of this genre – G.K.). Finally I repeat Turnbull's remarks on kinship amongst the Mbutis: 'With the best will in the world, it is not possible to apply the kind of analysis suggested by Lévi-Strauss (1958), to the Mbuti (1966:238)'.

A more likely, historical explanation for the origin and continuity of kinship and lineage systems has been proposed by C.E. Joel in *New Diffusionist* (1970, Nos. 1 and 3). Referring to Hocart, (The Life-giving Myth-Ch. XXII), Joel attributes them to the emergence of early kinship when royal family relationships began to play an important part, involving royal succession with its transfer of power and prestige and the inheritance of property. Joel (1970:87) points out that these and related factors arouse the strongest passions in every society. These originally restricted kinship relations became modified in the course of time as they devolved down to more primitive, semi-civilized, sedentary and pastoral client groups.

This assessment finds support in a detailed examination of kinship and lineage principles. In Macmillan (1983:183), it is pointed out that 'among the central components of kinship are grant and social paternity for the purpose of inheritance'. It is also stated that Radcliffe-Brown and Fortes in their kinship theories stress inheritance and succession (p.184). Goody suggests that descent theories use examples involving homogenous transmission of property after death. (p. 184).

As to lineage relations (Macmillan p. 209), it is stated that 'in principle, patrilineal systems depend upon the passing of status and property from father to legitimate son; and in matrilineal systems inheritance is traced from the uncle to nephew'. Thus the entire field of kinships and lineages is permeated by property, status and inheritance. Such conditions apply however solely to property-owning sedentary and pastoral societies, which only emerged in the wake of food production. They are, in terms of total hominid history, a rather novel and recent phenomenon. The circumstances of their appearance will be treated in more detail in my second volume (in preparation).

In summary, the conditions which form the basis of kinship and lineage structures can certainly not apply to culturally ultra-primitive food-gathering groups, to whom landownership, inheritance of property, and private property itself (beyond modest personal possessions) means nothing.[4]

In conclusion, 'Structuralism' suffers from some of the same weakness as cultural evolutionary theories. It is unable to rationally explain the independent emergence of cultural parallels in a world-wide context, be they of a material, ideational or institutional nature. This theme will be further explored in volume two.

5. THE FUNCTIONALIST APPROACH

Functionalism is to an extent interwoven with structuralism, insofar as it attempts to explain the functions of countless social phenomena and their structures, though not necessarily following Malinowski or Lévi-Strauss. Social anthropologist Leach (1970:9), writes: 'I myself was once a pupil of Malinowski, and I am at heart still a "functionalist" even though I recognize the limitations of Malinowski's own brand of theory. Although I have occasionally used the "structuralist" methods of Lévi-Strauss to illuminate particular features of particular cultural systems, the gap between my general position and that of Lévi-Strauss is very wide'.

What distinguishes functionalism is its emphasis on 'need'. As Freud remarked to his friend Ferenzci (Jones: 1961:442): 'Our intention is to place Lamarckism entirely on our basis and show that '*need*', which creates and transforms organs is nothing other than the power of unconscious ideas over the body'. As it happens, Malinowski, one of the founders of Functionalism, fully agreed with this point of view. In an article in *Psyche* (1923:293:322) entitled 'Psychoanalysis and Anthropology' he wrote: 'By my analysis, I have established that Freud's theories not only roughly correspond to human psychology, but that they follow closely the modifications in human nature brought about by various constitutions of society'. (my emphasis)

The central tenet of the Functionalist School, as proclaimed by Malinowski is that

> every institution or custom has a function in the society in which it occurs and that all the institutions cohere to make a viable unit, or even organism. This functioning was further the raison d'etre of the institution and eventually, by implication the 'cause' of the institution, which by now had come to be regarded as meeting a 'need', biological, psychological or social or a combination of all three. Thus the various customs and behaviours and beliefs of these societies met various needs arising from the essential nature of men living

in association. The needs were those of the group here and now, metabolism, reproduction, bodily comforts, etc.

... and the cultural responses to these were, according to Malinowski,

commissariat, kinship, shelter, etc., which comprised the customs and institutions and beliefs of the group. These were of here and now and not dependent upon, or the consequences of, past situations, historical circumstances, for their existence or their characteristics (Malinowski, 1922, 1944).

Lewis (1976:55) comments: 'The functionalist method which Malinowski so strenuously championed amounted, in fact to little more than acknowledging that every custom or institution, however strange and bizarre, served some contemporary (i.e., useful) purpose'.

Durkheim, another prominent functionalist, developed a theory of religion which identified it with social cohesion: 'religious beliefs and rituals are understood in terms of the role they play in promoting and maintaining social solidarity, while Radcliffe-Brown argued that religious ceremonial, promotes unity and harmony and functions to enhance social solidarity and the survival of society. Malinowski again, saw religion and magic as assisting the individual to cope with situations of stress and anxiety (Macmillan, 1983:139).

According to Lewis (1976:48), Durkheim went so far as to assert that crime was necessary and useful to society (i.e., had a useful function). The punishment that followed was shown as a collective revenge of society on the criminal, thus symbolically reaffirming and restoring the moral values and common loyalties which the criminal had desecrated: 'It was a symbolic lynching in which an outburst of punitive indignation healed the injuries which the criminal had inflicted on society'. Durkheim implied that a certain amount of crime might even be necessary to keep society in a healthy state; thus elevating criminals to the status of public benefactors. These and other functionalist views greatly resemble those of Dr. Pangloss, in Voltaire's *Candide*, whose philosophy was based on the contention that we live in the best of all possible worlds, with everything connected and arranged for the best. This is not necessarily an exaggerated comment on functionalist ideas, in so far as Durkheim even maintained that war and nationalism were good, because they stimulate individuals to display their most heroic virtues, thereby creating unity and purpose (I.M. Lewis, 1976:53).

It is in this manner that the functional 'need' (or usefulness) of such social elements as kinship and lineage structures, magic and religion, and even crime and war is explained; the guiding motif being allegedly the achievement of social cohesion and harmony. This principle of functionalist 'need' was also introduced into material culture, with some functionalists, maintaining that occupations such as the fashioning of stone tools, spinning and weaving, pottery and agriculture, and even civilization itself came about because they were needed when societies reached certain stages of development.

Generally, the functionalist principle of 'need' can be refuted by noting firstly that (contrary to the proverb), 'Necessity *is not* the mother of invention', and even an obvious need will often remain unfulfilled due to blinkered imagination. Secondly, even if a useful innovation is made it may frequently be ignored, due to the human tendency to adhere to traditional ways.

There is no better example than the Fuegian inhabitants of the Tierra del Fuego at the southernmost part of South-America. When Darwin encountered them in the last century he found them stark naked, despite living in a climate which was harsh and inhospitable, and despite the obvious need to protect themselves from the seasonably wintry weather with some covering. Furthermore, at one time or the other they were in contact with neighbours who wore protective clothing but the Fuegians did not follow their example. This is certainly a case where the principle of 'need' was most blatantly ignored.

Since the art of making fire dates back at least 1$\frac{1}{2}$ million years, it ought to be expected that all present people should have acquired this skill. However, according to Forde (1968:141), the Bora and Japura people of Brazil, as well as the Mbuti of the Congo, were, before they knew of matches, ignorant of methods of making fire.

In a similar vein, pottery-making is a world-wide craft known perhaps for 10,000 years. Yet the Blackfoot Indians of Central North-America had no pottery until a few years ago, and used hide-pouches in place of cooking pots (Forde, 1968:63). Equally, the Mbuti, as described by Turnbull, were devoid of any knowledge of pottery making.

Other examples where functionalist theory founders is the loss of useful skills. Forde (1968:430) has pointed out that rice and millet cultivation was known by some of the ancestors of the Polynesians, but it was later abandoned. And he adds: 'This would be no more surprising than the probable abandonment of both potmaking and weaving'.

W.H.R. Rivers who did extensive fieldwork in the Pacific wrote in great detail about the abandonment of 'Canoe Making' in the Torres Islands, off N. Australia (1926: pp.191/196); and the loss of 'Pottery Making' in Polynesia; and that of the 'Bow and Arrow' as a hunting weapon in many parts of New-Guinea, especially among the people who speak proto-Melanesian languages. Bow and arrow are now only used as toys. It was this comprehensive study of *The Disappearance of Useful Arts* which persuaded Rivers to reject the 'Independent Invention Theory in Culture'. Rivers caused a sensation in 1911, when in an address to the British Association on the topic of 'The Ethnological Analysis of Culture' he announced his conversion to the historical, diffusionist interpretation of so-called primitive cultures. 'The choice in Ethnology', he said, 'is between accepting diffusion, or the confusion of Bastian'. Far from his diffusionist conversion diminishing his prestige, he was called upon in 1922 to assume the Presidency of the Royal Anthropological Institute, still considered the highest honour in British anthropology. Unfortunately he died suddenly before taking office. Had he survived, British anthropology might have taken a different course.

To quarrel with functionalism one need not deny that social phenomena can have beneficial functions, just as most products of material culture are useful. Objectionable are some of the means by which functionalists try to explain the independent origin of identical cultural phenomena and products, when found in distant parts of the world, attributing them to psychological factors common to all mankind, i.e., Bastian's 'psychic unity'.

Malinowski was a leading exponent of such thinking. In his book *A Scientific Theory of Culture* (1944), he presents us with a veritable eulogy of Frazer whom he describes as one of the world's greatest teachers and masters on the subject (though he remarks that few of his other theoretical contributions are acceptable today). Malinowski points out that Frazer was essentially addicted to psychological interpretations of human belief and practice (p.188), and also, 'Frazer believes in the essential similarity of the human mind and human nature.[1] He sees clearly that "human nature" has to be assessed primarily in terms of human needs' (p.212).

'A host of writers', writes Malinowski, 'such as Wundt and Crawley, Westermarck and Lang, Frazer and Freud, have approached fundamental problems such as origins of magic and religion, of morals and totemism, of taboo and mana, by propounding exclusively psychological solutions'. Furthermore, according to Malinowski, 'Freud took his anthropological evidence from Frazer'. Neither does Malinowski forget E.B. Tylor (the father of unilinear cultural evolutionism), noting that Tylor's minimum definition of religion and his whole theoretical concept of animism was that the essence of primitive faith and philosophy, was primarily psychological'.

And while Malinowski shows little enthusiasm for Frazer's other, purely theoretical contributions (p.19), his views about the psychological origin of cultural phenomena, matches those of Frazer, Tylor and Freud. In the following we recall (see p.22) Freud's words on the subject and Malinowski's compliance with them. Freud: 'Our intention is to place Lamarckism entirely on our basis and show that "need", which creates and transforms organs, is nothing other than the power of unconscious ideas over the body ...'; and Malinowski: 'By my analysis, I have established that Freud's theories roughly correspond to human psychology, and that they closely follow the modifications in human nature brought about by various constitutions in society'.

What we find here is nothing less than a complete surrender to Bastian's principle of the 'Psychic Unity of all Mankind'.

Again the matter is explainable only on the basis of Lamarckian inheritance, in an all-pervading unilinear cultural process. As shown above, Freud endorsed Lamarckism (now considered erroneous) and its part played in social theory. On the other hand, most modern social anthropologists, while continuing to use the same Freudian approach in their social theories, tend to overlook its Lamarckian basis.

6. THE CONCERNS OF SOCIAL ANTHROPOLOGY

In the strict sense of the meaning, 'society' or 'social life' as dealt with by contemporary social anthropology is a relatively recent historical phenomenon. It began when culturally developing human groups formed sedentary communities exceeding in numbers the extended families or bands of hunter-gatherers. What we find, after about four million years of a culturally more or less simple hunter-gatherer existence, is the first appearance of sizeable social units in a mainly agricultural context about 10,000 years ago.

It is likely that even earlier Neanderthal cave, or tent-dwellers, formed already what may be called 'tribal societies'. Equally so, large scale pre-agricultural sedentary food-collecting settlements may have existed in Jericho and elsewhere. But we know nothing of either's internal social organization or customs. On the other hand, the societies, clans or tribes which form the main study objects of social anthropologists are hardly older than 6000 years, if that. *Macmillan's Student Encyclopaedia of Sociology* (1983), confirms this since none of the subjects indexed has any connection with a pre-agricultural mode of life. The terms hunter-gatherer, or gatherer-hunter are not listed, and the book's sociology or social-science is almost exclusively concerned with sedentary societies.

A close study of culturally simple hunter-gatherers, in their natural state (as yet little influenced by their culturally more advanced neighbours), finds mainly simple family ties, which as in any healthy family today, are based on love, affection, companionship, and above all, sharing.[1] However, such pristine conditions ceased when some of these groups or bands adopted agriculture.[2] An increased food supply led to the larger social groupings of tribal societies, villages and towns and eventually states and nations. In such novel situations, new sets of personal relations (now called social relations), had to be arbitrarily arrived at to keep order, representing an entirely novel and artificial state of affairs, not being quite compatible with man's basic instincts and aspirations, which biologically seen are more suited to a simple family life within the confines of small groups.

Elsewhere we shall endorse the view that civilization arose from special historical events connected with big river irrigative agriculture; and that the corresponding social situation led to the emergence of kingship, godhead and organized religion, followed by a host of subsidiary institutions, customs and rituals.

It is surmised that this ancient Egyptian or Sumerian model of 'Urban Literate Civilization' with all its ramifications, subsequently became the catalyst from which later civilizations, and their client groups, drew their cultural, and even more, their social heritage, although with adaptations and transformations to fit new conditions and needs. In addition, the system found its imitators in the more primitive food-producing tribal societies forming on the fringes of early civilizations. Here the original customs and institutions underwent many changes, and in their new adulterated state led to aberrations, in customs and behaviour, which nowadays, seem to defy logical explanation. Yet many modern social anthropologists ascribe these aberrations to inborn tendencies of a psychological nature and ignore the very real possibility of historical explanation. In any case, these more primitive, semi-civilized, tribal groups, surviving in various forms into the present, have become the favoured hunting-ground and object study of social anthropologists.

To sum up – social organization, going beyond extended family groups or bands (i.e., hunter-gatherers), is arbitrary, and not necessarily, logical or common sense. It stems from historical association, thereafter being passed on from generation to generation, by habit, tradition or by simple inertia sometimes with no apparent benefit or purpose. Its expressions include initiation ceremonies, human and animal sacrifice, cannibalism, witchcraft, sorcery, totem and tabu, couvade, the seclusion of young girls for months and even years at the advent of puberty, ritual murder, the extension of earlobes, the chiselling of holes into the 'living' skull (trepanning), the ritual removal of an adult's front-teeth, and the barbaric act of female circumcision. The fact that these and other social customs find their parallels in many parts of the world, points to common historical sources, a conclusion which will be more closely examined in a sequel to this treatise.

It is precisely because such parallels have been ascribed to inborn human psychology (the psychic unity of all mankind), that social theories of unilinear and multilinear evolution, functionalism and structuralism, and other conceptions, inspired by Bastian, Freud, Frazer, Tylor, and taken up by Lévi-Strauss, Malinowski, Steward, Glyn Daniel, and others, have been concocted.

It would even seem that human expansion beyond family groups or bands of food-gatherers and the subsequent attempt to cope with the complexities of social life in an ever expanding world population have added unprecedented difficulties to human biological existence. This has now culminated in a world of separate sovereign nations plagued by countless conflicts and wars. The crediting of these new and larger social assemblages (which are hardly 6000 years old) and thus represent less than 1/600th of human existence, as being ordained by fixed laws, is one of the great paradoxes of so-called social science. Even more so, the idea that these artificially assembled social groups (the family-plus), are ruled by social laws which stem from an inborn psychology, is an almost pathological obsession currently prevalent amongst large sections of social anthropologists.

139

CONCLUSION

The purpose of the present study has been to show that the evolutionary (psychological) interpretation of cultural phenomena is outdated. In contrast, an evaluation of accumulated fossil evidence, particularly in relation to its cranial aspect, points to an historical diffusionist interpretation.

In examining current anthropological theories such as cultural multilinealism (which can be shown to be merely another form of discarded unilinealism), structuralism and functionalism, we find them all linked to the now outdated concept of cultural evolution, which in turn is again based on the psychologically linked thesis of the equal working of the human mind. This latter concept was originally formulated by Bastian and further developed by Morgan, Tylor, Frazer, Freud and others. Furthermore, all of these theories are rooted in Lamarckian heredity, an observation which finds prominent exposition in the ethnological writings of Sigmund Freud, who admits being a convinced Lamarckist.

What needs stressing here is that conventional social anthropology which draws its study material almost exclusively from sedentary societies, (while disregarding hunter-gatherer history), is principally linked to the above mentioned cultural evolutionary theories. Yet simple hunter-gatherer societies have occupied our earth for four million years or more, some of them even surviving into our age while in contrast, the more culturally complex agriculturally based sedentary societies are at best only 10,000 years old, representing thus a mere 0.25% of total human history, or 2% of the duration of Homo sapien's presence, whose age is about 300,000 years.

The rare example of the surviving, culturally ultra-primitive Mbuti hunter-gatherers of the Ituri Forest of Zaire, gives us a possible clue to the life-style of hunter-gatherers throughout the preceding four million years of human pre-agricultural exis-

140

tence. Their social life has been described by Colin Turnbull as being free of most of those social customs and institutions which have become part and parcel of more complex sedentary societies, principally those of a tribal character. These customs and institutions can be enumerated as: hierarchical status relations with chiefs, headmen and councillors; complicated kinship rules; mythical accounts; totems and taboos; rituals of initiation, marriage and burial; ancestor worship; superstitious beliefs in magic, witchcraft and sorcery; trepanning; circumcision; cannibalism; human-sacrifice; all kinds of religious practices and more. As to their communal behaviour, the Mbuti, when remaining undisturbed by external influences, lead a perfectly peaceful existence, and show no aggressive tendencies.

In comparison, the more complex sedentary tribal societies, during their relatively short history, have become saddled with the above mentioned medley of social customs and institutions, and are prone to aggression as well as being riddled by internal and external conflicts. Also worth mentioning is that the conditions which apply to human total history, also logically apply to the entire history of Homo sapiens, whose total food-gathering sequence stretches over 300,000 years (minus the last ten thousand years of sedentary life – apart from some surviving hunter-gatherers). Fossil evidence shows that during Homo sapien's entire life-span, which includes modern humans, there occurred no significant biological change either in his physical or mental makeup. This means that also his psychological aptitudes must have remained basically unchanged during the entire period.

It is therefore inconceivable to accept the notion that while the psychological aptitudes of Homo sapiens remained unchanged over 300,000 years (minus the last ten thousand years), there could have occurred during the last ten thousand years a tremendous psychological upsurge, leading to the spontaneous world wide emergence of the above mentioned medley of customs and institutions, all of them being allegedly induced by a cultural evolutionary process.

The survival of the culturally unsophisticated Mbuti, alone, who are recognized as fully fledged Homo sapiens, (being free

141

of the above mentioned medley of customs and institutions) already proves the absurdity of the above culturally evolutionary assertion and its alleged psychological consequences. The further claim that identical cultural parallels found elsewhere in the world, are, and can have been, the result of spontaneously produced independent developments, as part of an evolutionary process, induced by an inborn psychology, must also be discarded.

I suggest therefore that the rational alternative to outdated cultural evolutionism, is an historically based diffusionist interpretation of cultural events. This suggests further that the emergence of cultural elements and phenomena in human history is in the first place due to local origin (or, in a wider aspect, due to specific historical circumstances), while their parallel appearance elsewhere is due (with few exceptions), to a process of spread or diffusion from an original source. And such a process can be postulated irrespective of whether physical contact can be proved or not. A typical example of this is the origin and spread of the great religions of this world, and even more so that of the origin and world wide spread of Western Civilization. The second volume to follow will produce additional evidence for the diffusionist interpretation of humankind's cultural history.

NOTES

PART I

Preface

1. Generally speaking, human culture as proposed here (while not rejecting alternative definitions) embraces four main aspects: (a.) Material Culture: Technology; (b.) Personal and Group Inter-Relations: Sociology; (c.) Belief Systems: Religion and Ideology; (d.) The Arts. Part I, deals mainly with (i), the other parts emphasize (ii) and (iii), while (iv) plays an altogether subsidiary role.

Chapter 1

1. Tobias concludes: 'There is still much uncertainty and disagreement about the relationship between the anatomically modern *Homo sapiens* who seems to have emerged in the African continent (there is some recent evidence of an early manifestation at Qafzeh in Israel) – and the earlier *Homo sapiens* who was at that time already in existence in Africa, Europe and Asia. The Mitochondrial DNA (EVE hypothesis) seems to suggest that this group of people arising in the African continent spread all over the world and superseded or wiped out all previous forms of early *Homo sapiens*, possibly blending partly with them. This is so highly inconceivable a situation that many of us have been most hesitant to accept the EVE hypothesis. Further evidence is awaited'.

Chapter 2

1. Referring to the evolutionary transmission from H. erectus to H. sapiens for which he allocates a space of 500,000 years, P.V. Tobias remarks (1985b), 'This phase of hominidisation is bedeviled with so many problems of definition and of morphological appraisal that estimates of dating vary from 0.75 to 0.25 B.P.'.

143

Chapter 4

1. The earliest example of the possible use of a wooden spear comes from Clakton, eastern England. It is that of a spear-tip (likely from a thrusting spear), 300,000 years old. A similar later find c. 120,000 years old has been reported from Lehringen in Germany (J. Gowlett, 1984).

2. George Carter describes the 'bola' as a key weapon of early man. He informs me (personal communication, 1939) – 'With it man can take on anything up to an elephant'. A band of men, each with a bola, would be too formidable for anything except the largest predator to tackle. It has been found at the bottom of Olduvai, in China by 1 million B.P., in Calico (now dated at 200,000 B.P.) and is used all over North and South America. It is still in use marginally in Africa, China and in contemporary South America.

3. Rounded stones possibly for reducing coarse foods appear at the base of Olduvai Gorge (Carter 1973 b:3).

4. R.J. Clarke (Dart Symposium, 1985) has described Acheulian cleavers and hand-axes, found at Sterkfontein, older than 1.5 million years.

Chapter 5

1. According to R. Leakey the Neanders produced upwards to 60 identifiable items – mostly finer and more precise than Acheulian tools or anything in preceding cultures.

2. In order to reduce the long word Neanderthaler, I am substituting it occasionally by the term *Neander*.

Chapter 6

1. This opinion is shared by P.V. Tobias. In the Introduction to his book *The Brain in Hominid Evolution* (1971), he speaks of the comments of the distinguished neuro-anatomist, Dr. Gerhardt v. Bonin, who, after a lifetime of studies of brain and endocasts concludes, 'It should at least be admitted that most of what has been said and written on the sulci of the brain as they have been seen on endocasts is worth very little. A view shared by not few of those mentioned above: (i.e., Le Gros Clark, Cooper and Zuckermann 1936, Edinger 1948, Conolly 1950, Simon 1965, and Banchat and Stephan 1967'.

2. Reticulate (or network) evolution, as indicated by Julian Huxley (1963), specifically in humans, results from cross-mating in face of differences in colour, appearance and behaviour. In other words, it resembles racial intermarriage.

3. Latest available life-expectancy figures issued by the World Health Organisation are as follows: average for developing countries is now 59.7 years compared to 41 years four decades ago. During the same period life-expectancy in China and East Asia rose from 42.7 to 69.9 years; and in Africa from 38 to 51.9. In South and central America the comparable figures are 51.2 to 66 years, (W.H.O. 24 Sept., 1989).

4. One prominent critic commenting on the above has observed that he cannot see why increasing knowledge replaces the need for increased intelligence. He says it can be argued that with the great expansion in the amount and complexity of information, more, not less intelligence is needed in order to make use of it.

My response is that there are two sides of intellectual evaluation; one, the already available genetically inborn potential, and two, the possibility of making greater use of something which is possibly under-used. Hence, modern life with its greater intellectual demands in the fields of science and technology is already adequately served by making greater use of an already inborn intellectual potential. Furthermore, an increasing availability of information also eases the task. All this can be accomplished without any biologically based selective process in this direction, which, as we well know, does not operate in modern life.

To illustrate the above, I may refer to a remark, made by a South-Sea Islander, to Margaret Mead: 'My father was a cannibal, but I am going to be a doctor'. Thus bridging in one generation a cultural gulf of millennia, without any genetical adjustment.

5. The brain coefficient is a figure obtained by dividing the brain size in cm3 by the body's height in centimetres.

6. A significant comment in this respect appeared on the Science page of the *International Herald Tribune*, March 15, 1990. It reads:- 'CHANGES IN GENES: NOW DOUBTS ARISE: Scientists have challenged an unconventional idea that bacteria could purposefully alter their genes in beneficial ways.

A little over a year ago researchers at the Harvard School of Public Health published results from experiments that found that strains of E-coli bacteria that were unable to digest sugars acquired the ability to do so when sugar was the only source of energy available. The researchers caused a sensation by suggesting that mutations may not always be random, an idea contrary to a fundamental tenet of genetics. Cells may have mechanisms for choosing which mutations will occur.' John Cairns, Julie Overbough and Stephan Miller wrote in their paper, published in the Sept. 8, 1988, issue of the journal *Nature*, 'Now in Nature's March 8 issue, John E. Mittler and Richard E. Lenski of the University of California at Irvine, reject that proposition. They conducted similar experiments and found that the rate of mutation increased when the cells were starving whether or not the sugars that would benefit them were present.'

Chapter 7

1. At the Third International Conference on Hunter-Gatherers (Carmen Shrire, 1983), a majority view concluded that there were two different types of hunter-gatherers, primary and secondary ones. The primary type embodies those groups who do appear to be the aboriginal, autochthonous peoples of their respective regions of whom there exist at present no cultural, historical, or linguistic evidence of a prior agricultural adaptation; while the secondary type appears to derive from sedentary agricultural people representing essentially a re-adaptation.

2. This category includes the Veddahs of Ceylon: Andamanese aborigines; the Sakai and Jakun, the Australoid neighbours of the Semang, a proto-Malay people; certain Negrito peoples of the Philippines; the Arunta and other aborigine peoples of Australia. In the Americas they include peoples such as the Dene, Salish, Paiute, and the Indian peoples of California; further south there are numerous Brazilian peoples, while in the Chilean parts there still linger the Fuegians and their close neighbours the Chonoans, and the Onas. In the arctic regions we encounter various Eskimo peoples of different complexion with an economy partly based on fishing and

hunting. All of these above mentioned can only nominally be considered as genuine (bona-fide) hunter-gatherer people.

3. It appears that the use of fire was very sporadic throughout the ages and by no means universal. Daryl Forde has recorded (1968:141) that the Boro and other Japura people in Brazil are even today totally ignorant of any method of fire-making, and according to Turnbull (1966); so too were the Mbuti of the Congo. Writing of the absence of all knowledge of fire-making (except after acculturation), Turnbull relates that each household maintains its own hearth. When on trail embers are usually carried by women. Matches are rarely used as they become quickly damp and useless, even if available.

4. According to Turnbull (1966), older Mbuti assert that fire-hardened spears are effective even against the largest game. The same applies to arrows, preferring fire-hardened wood-points, in using their poisoned arrows. Having no knowledge of metal-working (except on later acculturation), the Mbuti entirely depend on the village for all metal goods. There is absolutely no knowledge of pottery making.

5. This ought to include the 'bola'. (See also footnote (2), Chapter 4.)

Chapter 8

1. This development is described by Clark/Piggott (1970), 'The earliest assemblages comprise pebbles flaked into the form of choppers from one direction. In the second phase uni-directional flaking is still predominant, but this is supplemented by work from two directions and applied to a wider range of shapes. Phase three is marked, above all, by the predominance of bi-directional flaking. Finally, the primitive pebble forms are supplemented by others flaked on both faces, precursors of the bifacially flaked tools of the succeeding Middle Pleistocene'. From this brief account it is plain that *evolution* (read 'develop-ment') (my emphasis) *was extremely slow*, since on any of the accepted chronologies it was spaced out over a period running into hundreds of thousands of years.

2. C. Coon has written (1967), that 'The most striking fact about these hand-axes is that wherever they are found they

follow the same sequence of forms. During the quarter of a million years when men made these tools, the style changed very little, but what changes were made are to be seen everywhere. Even the most learned specialist in the archaeology of the Lower Palaeolithic, as the culture of this period is called, can distinguish an English hand-axe of a given age from one from Palestine or from South Africa only by variations in material and weathering'.

3. Darwin wrote (*Origin of Species*, 1859): 'The similar framework of bones in the hand of man, wing of bat, fin of porpoise, and leg of the horse – the same number of vertebra forming the neck of the giraffe and the elephant, and innumerable other such facts, at once explain themselves on the theory of descent with slow and successive modifications'.

Chapter 10

1. George Carter observes (1973b:4) All men were seed-gatherers for millions of years and were subject to environmental and population stress and almost all men had the metate for at least tens of millennia. Yet at most, in only a few spots, and in terms of the time scales we are dealing with, *at about the same time*, men suddenly undertook the domestication of plants. Why if the need, opportunity and focus of interest had existed for millions of years, and the human ability (*Homo* with brain capacities approaching ours) had existed for about half a million years should this rush of domestication have burst out all over the globe like an epidemic of measles? Was it indeed like measles, a communicable disease?

2. George Carter in 'A Hypothesis Suggesting a Single Origin of Agriculture', published 1977 in *Origin of Agriculture*, by Charles A. Reed (Aldane, Chicago pp. 83–133), came to similar conclusions. Carter argued that potential domestic plants are ubiquitous, but only a few plants were originally chosen and the New World plants mimic the Old World domestics. The whole thing happened world-wide at the same time (give or take a couple of thousand years). Carter remarks that the idea of a possible single origin goes back to G. Eckholm who muted it 25 years earlier.

Chapter 11

1. At Catal Hüyük rooms of modest size have been excavated (decorated with bulls-heads), which have been described as temples.

2. Also at Catal Hüyük there are several statues of big females sitting on thrones who have been called Mother or Fertility Goddesses.

3. Mellaart, discoverer and excavator of Catal Hüyük wrote (1965:75): 'The neolithic civilization (read pre-civilization, G.K.) revealed at Catal Hüyük, shone like a super-nova ... it burned itself out and left no permanent mark on the cultural development of Anatolia after 5000 B.C'.

4. S. Lloyd and F. Safar (1981), point out that 'the first human settlement was located at a site now called Tell Abu Sharein. It was a high dune of wind drifted sand, possibly forming an island in a wide area of marshland once a tidal lake at the head of the Persian Gulf '.

Appendix

1. G. Montgomery, in the journal 'Discover' in an article 'Molecules of Memory', relates the following interesting facts: 'The animal that lets us in on the arcane secrets of memory is the California marine snail whose remembrances of things past would normally consist of little more than mating and munching seaweed. Kandel has made the large, shell-less sea slug *Aplysia california* a super-star within the neuroscientific community.

His choice of a mere mollusk stems in part from his belief that the ability to store information is an evolutionary legacy, a universal feature of the nervous system: many invertebrate animals and all vertebrates are capable of primitive forms of learning and remembering. Because of this common evolutionary heritage, the reasoning goes, memory and learning in slugs and people are likely to have common cellular features. *Aplysia*, of course, possesses far fewer nerve cells than we do - a mere 20,000 or so. And *Aplysia's* neurons are larger. Otherwise however, its neurons are hardly distinguishable from our own; their structure and signalling mechanisms are the same ('Discover', Dec. 1989, pp.46/55, New York).

2. G. von Bonin, 1963.

PART II

Foreword

1. By describing the First Category of hunter-gatherers at times as cultural primitives or even ultra-primitives, I am contrasting them with the more acculturated hunter-gatherers, placed in the Second and Third Categories, who live culturally more complex and sophisticated lives. It needs, however, stressing that the connotation 'primitive', as applied here, does not mean cultural inferiority or deficiency in intellect.

Chapter 1

1. They can be enumerated as: hierarchical status relations with chiefs, headmen and councillors; complicated kinship rules; mythical accounts; totems and taboos; rituals of initiation, marriage and burial; ancestor worship; superstitious beliefs in magic, witchcraft and sorcery; trepanning, circumcision, cannibalism, human-sacrifice; all kinds of religious practices and more.

2. These latter groups have no chiefs or headmen, no councils or legal systems, no belief in super-natural sanctions, and practice of magic, witchcraft or sorcery. There are no initiation rites or complicated kinship systems and when left undisturbed their life is peaceful and non-aggressive.

3. Earliest mentioning of the Twa of the Congo comes from a letter of a Pharaoh of the 6th Dynasty: (c. 2360 B.C.) to his general Hechuf who brought a dancer back from a Congo expedition. The Twa are also mentioned by Herodotus (c. 500 B.C.), and Aristotle (c. 400 B.C.), (*African Pygmies*, 1986:346).

4. The Mbuti boys have no fear of breaking all the initiation rules imposed by their Bantu masters when they are absent. Under certain conditions they will adopt the Bantu's burial customs, because 'they, (the Bantus) will give them much food'.

5. One ought to comment here that the vagueness of such a doctrine clearly suggests long indoctrination by their Bantu masters, and hardly ideas of their own making. This can also be seen under the next heading, *Godhead*.

6. Today, decades later, between 100,000 and 200,000 Twa

survive in the African states of the Cameroons, Congo, Gabon, The Central African Republic, Zaire, Burundi, Equatorial Guinea, and Rwanda. As a people of the forest, the Twa have been rejected, ignored and exploited. Some have left their native milieu, tempted by the prospect of an easier life. They have inevitably encountered money, alcoholism and diseases they never knew before. It is a kind of life which alienates and destroys them. (Extract from a film review of 'Pygmies' in the Bangkok Post 11 September 1986).

7. R.L. Holloway, a world authority on brain evolution, commenting on surviving hunter-gatherers, wrote (1984:183): 'Were modern living human hunters and gatherers to be judged on the basis of stone tool technology alone, they would probably be considered less advanced "brain wise", than Neanderthalers'.

Chapter 2

1. Lamarck published his theory in 1809, the year Darwin was born.

2. When Alfred Russell Wallace questioned Darwin as to whether he would discuss 'Man' in the forthcoming *Origin*, Darwin replied: 'I think I shall avoid the subject as ... surrounded by prejudice. Though I fully admit ... it is the highest and most interesting problem for the naturalist'. (Francis Darwin Editions – from *The Life and Letters of Charles Darwin*, John Murray 1888, Vol 2, p. 6).

3. T.I. Dyer, (1890:247), wrote in *Nature*, 'Darwin's difficulty was exactly that of everyone else, for, in the absence of any knowledge of the mechanism of genetics, the inheritance in certain instances, of the effects of the "use and disuse of parts" and of the "direct action of external conditions" seemed plausible enough and was accepted by virtually all the leading biologists of the 1870s. Even Weismann (1882) still gave some credence to the "transforming influence" of "direct action"'.

4. Jung's *Analytical Psychology* (Macmillan:170), has been criticised as metaphysical and unscientific. According to Jung, (Macmillan:180): 'there is a deeper level (of the personality), namely the "collective unconscious", this being the collective beliefs and myths of the race to which the individual belongs,

termed "archetypes". On the deepest level some of these will be "universal archetypes" common to all humans'.

5. Even the late Arthur Koestler, an ardent Lamarckist, admitted that Lamarckism has never been able to provide a physiological explanation for the inheritance of acquired characteristics, (Janus, 1978:273).

6. Modern genetics and more so genetic engineering have increasingly shown that there is no mechanism in the gene equipment to accommodate any Lamarckian type of inheritance. Yet Neo-Lamarckists (like the modern creationists), having lately become quite vocal in the biological field, have tried every subterfuge to infiltrate some Lamarckian principles into the biological evolutionary pantheon. I frankly admit that there are certain aspects in organic evolution which so far have defied explanations based on natural selection alone. But even if there were other, yet unknown, influences involved besides natural selection to explain the transmutation of species, they certainly cannot be based on Lamarckian inheritance, and would still be subject to the discriminating agency of natural selection as the final arbiter.

7. Darwin's term 'natural selection', as he admitted (1958:82), can be seen as a misnomer, because it actually describes an act of 'natural elimination'. Darwin came upon his 'Theory of Natural Selection' by first observing how animal and plant breeders selected chosen specimen for further breeding, thereby improving the race. The idea followed that a similar process might occur in nature, and so in order to distinguish the natural process from deliberate selection he called it 'natural selection'. Darwin reasoned that while human manipulation was a deliberate act, nature's process was not selective but eliminative. Under the basic conditions of nature – including the Malthusian principle of proliferation of progeny and the subsequent struggle for existence – the lesser adapted specimen will be eliminated while the better adapted, or fitter, ones will survive. This eliminative aspect must be kept in mind whenever the term 'natural selection' is used. Sexual selection in animals as elucidated by Darwin is perhaps a borderline case.

8. It was Spencer and not Darwin who popularised the term

'evolution', using it for the first time in an article entitled 'The Ultimate laws of Physiology' in 1857. It was also Spencer and not Darwin who coined the phrase 'survival of the fittest' in his *Principles of Biology* (1866:444, originally published 1864).

Chapter 3

1. Chambers 20th Century English Dictionary (1960 Edition) defines the term 'super-organic' (which is the same as supra-organic-G.K.) as: 'above or beyond the organic, psychical, pertaining to higher organization'.

2. J.H. Steward's definition of 'Multilineal Cultural Evolution' (1955:19), reads as follows: 'Multilineal Evolution is not interested in particular cultures, but is interested in finding local variations and diversity, troublesome facts which force the frame of reference from the particular to the general; it deals only with those limited parallels of form, function and sequence which have empirical validity'. Altogether a truly Delphic phraseology.

3. Again in discussing the origins of American civilization, Glyn Daniel (1964:105), asserts that: 'it was in fact a tale of independent cultural evolution'.

4. I find it appropriate to include here some criticism by Colin Turnbull of the ethnological theories Steward put forward in his work *Theory of Culture Change* (Urbana, U.S.A., 1955). Turnbull points at: 'unsupported assertions, derived from a superficial treatment of the subject, based on incorrect information' (1966:277).

Chapter 4

1. Lévi-Strauss, the leading structuralist, assumes with Freud (Leach, 1970:57) that a myth is a kind of collective dream, and that it is capable (by the analysis of its elementary structure – G.K.) of revealing hidden meanings. According to Freud, myth expresses unconscious wishes which are somehow inconsistent with conscious experience. Leach (1970:105) further comments that it becomes increasingly difficult to understand just what Lévi-Strauss means by 'elementary structures'. Lévi-Strauss also assumes with Freud, (Leach 1970:57) that the

'incest taboo' is a kind of collective dream, and that it is the cornerstone of all human society.

2. Leach (1970:20) on Lévi-Strauss: 'Any evidence however dubious is acceptable so long as it fits with logically calculated expectations; but wherever the data run counter to the theory Lévi-Strauss will either bypass the evidence or marshall the full resources of his powerful invective to have the heresy thrown out'.

3. Leach, in a private communication informs me that he personally rejects the term 'ultra primitive', for describing culturally less complex societies or peoples.

4. Colin Turnbull (1966:238) writing about the social structure among the Mbuti of the Congo, has this to say: 'This band is the basic unit and its membership is influenced by economic rather than kinship considerations', and ... (1965) 'The Mbuti show no tendency to adopt or develop the more complicated forms of social organization possessed by their neighbours (i.e., their Bantu masters). When they do adopt some customs of their masters, they do so for purely opportunistic reasons'.

Chapter 5

1. Edmund Leach (in his *Golden Bough or Gilded Twig?*, 1961) commenting on this aspect of Frazer, rightly observed 'He (Frazer, G.K.) took over from Bastian the assumption that the fundamental psychology of human beings will be everywhere reflected by similar customary behaviours, or, conversely, that similar customs have always the same symbolic implications, regardless of the context in which they appear'.

Chapter 6

1. This does not exclude the possibility of infanticide among primitive hunter-gatherers, nor that of internal conflicts (even violent ones), and even aggression. But field workers who have lived among such primitive groups have confirmed that such incidents are rare and disagreements when occurring, are usually amicably resolved.

2. R. Leakey (1981:227), has pointed out that the principal reason for the Khoi's (S. African food-gatherers) gradual adoption of agriculture is due to pressure from the government.

BIBLIOGRAPHY

Bailey, Geoff, 1983. *Hunter Gatherer Economy in Prehistory*, Cambridge Univ. Press, England.

Buchanan, F.H., 1867. *Journey Through the Countries of Mysore*, Canara and Malabar.

Butzer: see Caldwell.

Caldwell, J.R., 1966. *New Paths to Yesterday*, Thames and Hudson, London.

Cavelli Sforza, L., 1986. *African Pygmies*, Academy Press, London.

Chambers, 1960. *20th Century English Dictionary*, W & R Chambers, London.

Clark, D., see Washburn.

Daniel, Glynn, 1971. *The First Civilizations*, Pelican (first published 1968).

1964. *The Idea of Prehistory*, Pelican.

Darwin, E. 1888. *The Life and Letters of Charles Darwin*, Vol. 2, Murray, London.

Darwin, C. 1958. *The Origin of Species*, World's Classics, Oxford University Press.

Dornan, S.S., 1925. *Pygmies and Bushmen of the Kalahari.*

Dyer, W.T.T., 1888. 'The Duke of Argyll and the New Darwinians', in *Nature* 247/248, England.

Dyer, W.T.T., 1890. (In *Nature* 1890:247), England.

Forbes, H.O., 1885. *A Naturalist Wandering in the Eastern Archipelago.*

Forde, D.C., 1968. *Habitat Economy and Society*, Methuen, London.

Fortes, Mayer, 1973. *Elliot Smith Symposium.* The Zoological Society of London.

Freeman, D., 1974. '*The Evolutionary Theories of Charles Darwin and Herbert Spencer*'. (*Current Anthropology* Vol. 15 No. 3, Sept.).

Freud, S., (See Jones, E.).

Goodrich, E.S., 1912. *The Evolution of Living Organisms*, Jack, London.

Gowlett, J., 1984. *Ascent to Civilization*, Collins, London.

Harris, M., 1972. *The Rise of Anthropological Theory*, Kegan Paul, London.

Hocart, A.M., 1941. *Kingship*, Watts, London.

Hocart, A.M., 1941. *The Life-Giving Myth*, see Joel 1970.

Holloway, R.L., 1984. '*The Poor Brain of H. Neanderthalensis*', in *Ancestors, the Hard Evidence*, Allan R. Liss, New York.

Hose, C., and MacDougall, W., 1912. *The Pagan Tribes of Borneo*.

Huxley, J., 1957. *Evolution in Action*, Montana Books, New Amer. Libr. New York.

Isaak, G.L., 1978. 'The Archaeological Evidence for the Activities of Early African Hominids' in *Early African Hominids* – (ed. C.J. Jolly), Duckworth, London.

Joel, C.E., 1970. (in *The New Diffusionist* Nos. 1 and 3) Grt. Gransden, England.

Joel, C.E., 1973. (in *The New Diffusionist* Nos. 9 and 3) Grt. Gransden, England.

Joel, C.E., 1981. (in *Historical Diffusionism* No. 33 Dec.), London, England.

Johanson, D.C., and Edey M.A., 1982. '*Lucy*': *The Beginnings of Humankind*, Granada Publishing Co. Ltd., England.

Jones, E., 1961. *The Life of Sigmund Freud*, Pelican.

Koestler, A., 1978. *Janus*, Hutchinson, London.

Kroeber, A.L., see Daniel, G., 1971.

Laufer, B., 1918. (*The American Anthropologist* 20, review of R.H. Lowie's *Culture and Ethnology*).

Leach, E., 1970. *Lévi-Strauss*, Fontana/Collins, London.

Leakey, M.D., 1971. *Olduvai Gorge Vol. 3. Excavations in Beds I and II.*

Leakey, R.E., and R. Lewin, 1979/1981. *People of the Lake*, Collins/(Penguin, England.

Leakey, R.E., 1981. *The Making of Mankind*, Michael Joseph, and Rainbow Publications, London and New York.

Lévi-Strauss, C., 1968. *Structural Anthropology*, Allen Lane, London.

 1962. *The Savage Mind*, Weidenfeld, London.

Lewis, I.M., 1976. *Social Anthropology in Perspective*, Pelican, Middlesex.

Lowie, R.H., 1940. *An Introduction to Cultural Anthropology*, Farrar and Reinhart, New York.

Lukes, St., 1975. *Emile Durkheim, His Life and Work.* Allen Lane, Penguin, Middlesex.

Macmillan's *Student Encyclopedia of Sociology*, 1983. London.

Malinowski, B., 1923. *'On Freud: Psychoanalysis & Anthropology'*, in *Psyche* 4.

 1944. *A Scientific Theory of Culture*, University North Carolina.

Morgan Lewis, (1877). *Ancient Society*, 1964 edition. Edited by L.A. White, Harvard University Press.

Morris, B., – in *MAN*, Dec. 1974:542/555, R.A.I. publication, London.

Parker, S.T., and Gibson, K.R. *'A Developmental Model for the Evolution of Language and Intelligence in Early Hominids'.* *The Behaviourial and Brain Sciences* 2, 367–381 (1979).

Piddington, R., 1957. *'Malinowski's Theory of Needs'.* in *Man and Culture*, R.W. Firth (ed), Routledge, London and New York.

Radcliffe-Brown, A.R., 1931. *The Social Organization of Australian Tribes*, Oceania Monograph No. 1.

Radcliffe-Brown, A.R., *The Andaman Islanders*, Cambridge.

Rivers, W.H.R., 1926. *Psychology and Ethnology*, Kegan Paul, London.

Schebesta, P., 1929. *Among the Forest Dwarfs of Malaya.*

Shrire, Carmen, 1983. *Past and Present in Hunter Gatherer Studies*, Academic Press, *'Third International Conference of Hunter Gatherers'* – Bad Homburg, W. Germany, 13–16 June 1983.

Smith, G.E., 1973. *Centenary Symposium*, Report, Zoological. Society. London.

Spencer, H., 1857. *The Ultimate Laws of Physiology.*

Spencer, H., 1866. *Principles of Physiology.*

Seligman, C.G., 1910. *The Melanesians of British New Guinea*, Cambridge.

Seligman, B.Z., 1911. *The Veddahs*, Cambridge.

Steward, J.H., 1953. 'Multilinear Evolution; Evolution and Process' in *Anthropology Today*, University of Chicago Press.

Steward, H.J., 1955. *The Theory of Culture Change*, Urbana, U.S.A.

Sunday Times, London, (8 October 1972).

Tobias, P.V., 1956. *On the Survival of Bushman in Africa.*

Tobias, P.V., 1983. *Recent Advances in the Evolution of the Hominids: With Special Reference to Brain and Speech*, Pontifical Academy of Sciences, Scripta Varia, Vol. 50 pp. 85–140.

Turnbull, C.M., 1966. *Wayward Servants, The Two Worlds of African Pygmies*, Eyre & Spottiswood, London.

1965. *The Mbuti of the Ituri Forest*, Eyre & Spottiswood, London.

Tylor, E.B., 1881. *Anthropology*, England.

Voltaire, 1954 (written in 1756). *Candide*, Penguin Classics, England.

White, L., 1959. *The Evolution of Culture*, McGraw Hill, New York.

Wolheim, R., 1971. *Freud*, Fontana/Collins, London.

Washburn, 1968. In Symposium, *'Man the Hunter'*.